START YOUR OWN
CONSULTING BUSINESS

Additional titles in Entrepreneur's Startup Series

Start Your Own

Entrepreneur
MAGAZINE'S

.::: STARTUP

START YOUR OWN
CONSULTING
BUSINESS

Fifth Edition

YOUR STEP-BY-STEP GUIDE
TO SUCCESS

The Staff of Entrepreneur Media, Inc. & Terry Rice

Entrepreneur Press®

Publisher: Entrepreneur Press
Cover Design: Andrew Welyczko
Production and Composition: Eliot House Productions

This publication is designed to provide accurate and authoritative information in regard to the subject
matter covered. It is sold with the understanding that the publisher is not engaged in rendering legal,
accounting, or other professional services. If legal advice or other expert assistance is required, the
services of a competent professional person should be sought.

Entrepreneur Press® is a registered trademark of Entrepreneur Media, Inc.

An application to register this book for cataloging has been submitted to the Library of Congress.

ISBN 978-1-59918-665-8 (paperback) | ISBN 978-1-61308-422-9 (ebook)

Contents

Chapter 10
Sales and Marketing 121

Chapter 11
Pitching and Proposals 141

Chapter 12

Your First Clients and Commitment to Excellence 153

Chapter 13

Scaling Success and Managing Employees 161

Chapter 14

Additional Revenue Streams 169

Chapter 15

The Game Within the Game 185

About the Author 189

Index 191

Preface

Being a consultant is in your bones. Why? Because you already have something I can't teach you in this book. You have knowledge that people are waiting for you to share, ambition to get that process started, and the opportunity to live life on your own terms while still being able to support yourself. In fact, everything you need to be successful—however you define it—is already within you. I'm just here to give you structure and amplify your innate capabilities and achievements.

Prior to the Covid-19 pandemic, I would walk to my office in Brooklyn every day. The majority of people were walking to the subway as they headed to their jobs in Manhattan. Most of them looked completely miserable. Mind you, it was usually 8 A.M. and they were about to get on a crowded subway train, but I'm sure it ran deeper than that. It is my assumption and my experience that they may have been marching toward a job that didn't inspire them, didn't pay them enough, or didn't express their genius. I daydreamed about standing near the subway entrance yelling, "Turn around! Come to my office! Let me help you!" That said, ignoring all the insane things you encounter on a daily basis is a base-level coping mechanism for most people who live in New York City, so I don't think that approach would have worked too well.

At the onset of the Covid-19 shutdown, that whole way of life changed. Millions of people found themselves working from home or, unfortunately, not working at all. Although we'll eventually settle into this "new normal," for some, I know the future will be drastically different from the past. I'm certain many people will realize how fragile their job security truly is, will want to spend more time on the relationships and activities that fulfill them, or will want to pursue deeper, more meaningful work.

I firmly believe becoming a knowledge-based entrepreneur working as a coach or consultant is the clearest path to establishing a sustainable lifestyle, reclaiming your time, and setting you up for financial freedom. It allows you to support yourself on your own terms and be granted the autonomy to explore your passions while expressing the value you have to offer to your defined audience.

I also know many people will embark on this path and eventually turn away because they're lacking the critical skills and resources needed to push through the challenges associated with launching a consulting business. The life they're pursuing may seem so far away but, in reality, they're just a few months and a few tips away from building a sustainable business. I don't want anyone to quit when they're so close to establishing this legacy for themselves and those they care about.

Here's why. In 2015, I started my own consulting firm with a focus on helping brands grow through digital marketing. I figured if I could do it while working at Adobe and Facebook, I could do it for myself, too. Does this sound familiar? But, when I worked for someone else I was being spoon-fed amazing opportunities, so I never considered how hard it would be to get clients on my own. I had a strong business background, but I wasn't actually prepared to run a business.

Initially, I made a lot of mistakes. I didn't have a real plan, other than to make money.

I did cold outreach without offering any value. I said "Yes!" to every prospect who approached me, and I didn't charge them nearly enough. I also worked way too many hours and neglected my health and personal life.

In short, I made things harder than they had to be, and I almost went back to working a 9-to-5 job. I'm glad I didn't.

These days, things are much different. I work about 30 hours a week. I don't do cold calls, but I'm frequently contacted by high-value clients that I genuinely like and can help. And the best part is, I do all this while still picking up and dropping off my kids at school every day.

My goal and the goal of this book is to help you avoid the pitfalls I initially made so you can find success on your own terms.

Starting a consulting business is challenging, but it doesn't have to be so confusing. I'm going to partner with you to walk you through all the steps you need to take and explain how to avoid many of the mistakes that I've made and observed.

Stories of Starting Out

So much goes into getting your consulting business off the ground. What's it really like? I asked some of my fellow consultants to answer the question: "What was the first six months of your business like? What challenges and achievements did you encounter?"

Their responses were powerful and encouraging. Here's just a small sample of what they said:

I started exploring my business while I in a full-time role, so there was a lot less pressure in the beginning. My day job tied very closely to my marketing work, so it was a natural extension. I knew that I wanted to work with smaller companies, so I spent time understanding how I could best serve them. The main challenges I experienced were around the "other stuff" like figuring out health-care options, setting up the business, taxes, how much time to spend on promotion/business development work, vs. the actual work. My biggest achievement was getting the opportunity to work with a startup accelerator in the food tech space. This allowed me a great testing ground to learn what founders needed and to gain new areas of expertise, as I worked to address obvious marketing questions, as well as completely new ones. Some challenges included deciding what projects I would take on and how involved I wanted to get. I did take on a few projects that didn't turn out to be a great fit, but it was excellent learning for me, as I moved forward.

· · ·

The first six months were both exciting and full of mistakes. We landed several new and larger clients but also experienced the pitfalls to not having a niche and being in sales mode 24/7. Personally, I learned about how to manage employees, something I had not done / had before, and that was a challenge in itself especially for solopreneurs diving into having a team or another employee on board.

· · ·

I was working in wealth management in multiple companies in NYC, then I moved to Los Angeles and worked for a friend to try to grow his business. I decided to go a different direction with the services I wanted to offer and use my experience to offer advanced strategy to all businesses, no matter what the size. I realize today it was the best choice I've made for me and my current and previous clients. The first six months going solo were frightening but also very exciting. I fortunately had just signed a new client and had them on a retainer, which made the transition easier.

· · ·

The first six months were about building processes, systems, product offerings, and relationships. I hit the ground running with my first paying client, but realized quickly how important it was to have systems in place to continue to generate repeatable income. It was also about building me: my confidence, personal brand, and voice. Owning that I am the person to do this work and honoring that the industry was ready for the change that I can offer.

· · ·

My first six months were spent on myself and on my existing network. I wanted to ROLE MODEL what I was coaching. So I spent time and resources on my own education and coaching. I then immediately took action on engaging with my existing network and telling them what I was doing, how it was unique to me (my story), how I could help them, and asked if they wanted the help. Numerous people within my existing network needed and wanted the services I offered. So, I was IN BUSINESS! A challenge was going down rabbit holes of tasks that where not necessary, at that point in my business. Another significant challenge is to think you have to be an expert or have everything READY or COMPLETE before you can START.

· · ·

I started Modern Digital because I was laid off three weeks before Christmas and decided I would pursue my dream of starting my own consulting company. When I first started, I took any and all business that would come my way.

I had a lot of challenges with understanding how to price myself and market myself. Since I had never had to do any sort of business development or sales or pitching, these were all new practices and processes that had to be developed in those first few months.

A lot of what I did in those first six months was getting my business set up as a business, such as setting up my LLC and getting my business license and figuring out how to create a contract and get paid. Everything got a little easier after this for six months, but I remember doing a lot of admin work vs. doing consulting work.

One thing is clear with all of these stories: Though the motivation may be different for every consultant, the common theme is that you need to set achievable goals that are centered on what you want to get out of the consulting experience.

What Are Your Goals?

By picking up this book, you decided to listen to the voice that tells you to make that pivot, and I'm glad you did. Before we continue, though, I want you to think about the vision you have for your personal and professional life.

Think about your short-term goals. Two years from now:

▶ What do you want your work environment to look like?

▶ What does it feel like to have complete control of your destiny?

▶ Will you work five days a week, or take a weekday off just to recover and focus on your personal interests?

▶ How will it feel to constantly have prospects reaching out to you, curious to know if you can help them?

▶ How do you feel now that you're being valued for who you are, as opposed to just what you do?

You're inches away from making this happen, from elevating your personal career goals as a consultant. And you're in good company. Here's a quick story to illustrate.

In January of 2018, I met Justin Doyle, a former investment banker who burned out after 15 years in the industry. This path led him to become an executive coach at Justin Doyle Executive Coaching (www.levelupwithjd.com) so he could help other people in the same situation. When we first met, Justin was making about $2,000 per month as a consultant. In 2019, he grossed $400,000. He didn't meet the right person or stumble across some magical opportunity. Instead, he consistently created content for his defined audience that positioned him as the obvious solution to their problems. That's it. No paid ads or major publications. Like I said, you're inches away from making your vision a reality.

What to Expect In This Book

Throughout this book you'll hear more about other consultants who started out exactly where you are right now. They had raw talent but needed to develop specific skills and tactics in order to reach their full potential.

The book you're holding will do the same for you. Through my own experience, in addition to teaching and interviewing hundreds of consultants, I've documented the process aligned with building or scaling a consulting practice. I call it the Five Pillars of Success:

1. *Clarity.* Determining who you can help, the services you offer, how much to charge, and why you're their obvious choice.
2. *Process.* Focusing on doing what you love by implementing routines, apps, and services to streamline your business process.
3. *Branding and Marketing.* Learning how to position yourself, provide value to your audience, and perform "passive prospecting" through in-person events, third-party webinars, written content, and podcast appearances.
4. *Pitching and Proposals.* Leveraging tactics and templates to make this part simple, pain-free, and predictable.
5. *Fulfillment.* Determining how to deliver on the promises you've made with a systematic approach from onboarding to relationship management.

I'll walk you through each of these steps and teach you how to develop a process for your audience as well.

To help illustrate some of these points, I'll include stories from other consultants and also introduce an avatar, Tina, who very much represents the journey you're on. Through her experiences, you'll follow the progression through the Five Pillars of Success.

For background, Tina was previously in charge of operations at a small tech company. They recently folded, leaving her with a small severance and the freedom to do whatever she wanted to do next. Tina thoroughly enjoys improving business processes by removing process defects. She has decided she wants to enable other small businesses to grow by implementing customer relationship management (CRM) systems. This will enable them to streamline their lead-generation activities, close more deals, and increase overall revenue.

By design, I chose an avatar that works with small businesses, which will make her experiences applicable to you whether you decide to work with individuals or organizations.

How to Get the Most Out of This Experience

I sincerely want you to be successful, but you'll need to put in the work, too. After you read this book, I don't want you to feel inspired but not take any action. Being a consultant is all about taking action, so I've included specific action items and templates to leverage so you can get the most out of the experience. This process is easy to understand, takes effort to implement, and is aligned with success. To me, that's the perfect combination. Why? Because so many people will quit because of the effort involved. If you start to feel this way, consider that a trigger to separate yourself from everyone else who would give up and go revert back to their previous situation.

As you read, I suggest that you create a proper outline to take notes as you go along and document the action items you need to complete on your consultant journey. This can be on your computer or in a notebook. You'll also want to access the tools, templates, and worksheets that accompany this book on my website at www.terryrice.co/bookresources.

These resources are designed to help streamline and accelerate your growth as a consultant.

By far, the most important resource for you to access is The One Page Business Plan for Coaches and Consultants. I strongly suggest reviewing this first, and creating yours as you progress through each chapter.

You'll also gain access to "Attract & Convert: How to Get More Coaching and Consulting Clients." This mini-course will play a vital role in helping you determine your target audiences and the services you provide.

I suggest accessing both of them before moving forward as it will provide a great deal of clarity.

Although you can't skip the part where you spend time figuring things out, this book will serve as your guide to success. Let's get started.

Is Consulting Right for You?

As I'm sure you've already heard, working as a coach or consultant can be an exciting and lucrative career. You have an opportunity to work with a variety of individuals and businesses, learning more with every engagement. To top it all off, you're in complete control of who you work with and when you work. Well, technically.

Although you have a great amount of flexibility with your schedule, you also need to spend time making sure that schedule stays full. Beyond that, unlike a traditional in-house job, you're always auditioning. One wrong move and the client could discontinue using your services. This pressure can easily lead to a constant state of fight-or-flight syndrome. That's not the way I want to live, and I'll teach you how you can avoid it as well.

While there's no magic formula to finding success, I'm going to provide you with some repeatable best practices based on my own experience and interviews conducted with several successful coaches and consultants. Through their stories and mine, you'll discover how to properly launch and scale your business. I'll also pass along suggestions for time-saving tools and resources that will help you do this in a more efficient manner. Beyond that, I'll reinforce the need to take care of your physical and mental health.

Before we get started, there are some important questions you need to consider.

Why Do You Want to Do This?

Working as a consultant can be extremely rewarding from a financial and personal standpoint, but it's also incredibly challenging.

Chances are, you don't have a huge backlog of clients ready to hire you. In addition to handling the administrative side of launching a business such as getting a website (yes, you need one), you'll also need to focus on securing clients. It's important to realize you may not be able to fully support yourself until several months after launching your business.

Beyond that, your job is to be the smartest person in the room, at least in regard to your area of expertise. This will require you to constantly stay on top of any relevant changes in your industry and get used to the pressure that comes from describing yourself as an expert.

That's all part of the process, so you'll need to focus on the outcome: a life of independence and purpose. Your job is to help people make progress toward their goals, which is why you're so valuable. Fortunately, you typically get to decide when and how to create that value. Do you want to work on weekends? Only at night? Are you offering services in person or will you connect with clients remotely? It's all up to you, so long as you can bring in enough clients and revenue to hit your goals.

Are You Truly an Expert?

Before moving forward, this moment of self-reckoning is crucial. One of the biggest issues I see in the coaching and consulting industry is the large number of people who present themselves as experts, when they're clearly not. At least not to a trained eye.

I often see this happen with social media consultants. They realize they're pretty good at getting likes and engagement on their personal feed, so they decide to offer it as a service to businesses. While their intentions may be in the right place, there's a big difference between getting likes for a picture of your lunch and being able to leverage social media to drive customers to that same restaurant.

Although you might be able to convince a few clients that you know what you're talking about, internally, you'll know you're just trying to maintain appearances. This is different from imposter syndrome, which is a psychological pattern in which an individual doubts their accomplishments, and has a persistent internalized fear of being exposed as a "fraud." You straight up should not be positioning yourself as an expert, at least not yet anyway.

There's nothing wrong with admitting that. It just means you have to put in more work before you can brand yourself as an expert. I'll explain how to do so in the coming chapters.

Once you become an expert, you'll be comfortable admitting you don't know the answer to every question a client may have. It's an ironically empowering moment, and I remember the first time it happened to me. I was working at Adobe as a search engine marketing consultant, which involved helping enterprise-level clients optimize their Google Ad campaigns. During one call, a client asked me a question I couldn't answer. I provided them with a few possibilities, but said I needed to do more digging. They kept persisting, asking what was going on and how to fix it. I finally said, "I'm not sure, but the longer I spend on the phone, the longer it's going to take me to figure it out." In retrospect, I could have said it in a more polite way. Fortunately, they got the point without being offended and let me get to work. A few hours later, I solved their problem.

Do You Have Enough Grit to Push Through Challenging Times?

As I've said, and will continue to say, this is an incredibly challenging industry. The value you provide is constantly being judged, and the decision doesn't always go in your favor. Your effort may not be immediately rewarded, but you still need to persist. How will you handle rejection? How will you stay motivated through periods of stagnation?

It helps to know this is all part of the process. You need to reach a point where committing to the process is its own reward.

When I first started my consulting business, I spent hours cold emailing other members of the Brooklyn Chamber of Commerce. I'd wake up at 5 A.M. and start writing bespoke emails that referenced exactly how I could help these organizations. Over the course of two weeks, I sent over 200 emails. I got four responses. One was a complete dud. Another company actually hired me! Two were from other consultants who passed along extremely valuable guidance at no cost.

In retrospect, the guidance I gained from those other two consultants was pivotal to the success I've been able to attain during my independent consulting career. I would have never gained this insight if I gave up after the first 50 or 100 emails didn't pan out. You shouldn't either.

Do You Have a Support System in Place?

You're most likely starting this as a solo venture, which can get lonely very quickly. You'll need some kind of support system to keep you motivated and centered.

Fortunately, I have my wife. On several occasions she's done more than her fair share so I could focus on building my business. She also passes along sincere encouragement during times when I really needed it. I understand this is a luxury not all of us have, so it's important to realize a support system doesn't necessarily involve people you interact with in person. You can get support from an online group, a good book, or an inspirational podcast.

One podcast I recommend is *The Side Hustle Show*, which is hosted by Nick Loper. His podcast highlights the ideas, actions, and results you need to start and grow a successful business. Although you may not directly align with some of the businesses being featured, through their stories, you'll understand you aren't the only one who struggles.

No matter which route you choose, developing and leveraging a support system is an absolute necessity. Entrepreneurship is exciting, but it can and will get lonely.

Do You Truly Enjoy Helping People?

Sure, it's nice getting paid for doing a good job, but that's often not enough. If you truly enjoy helping people reach their goals, you'll receive a financial *and* intrinsic reward.

You'll quickly realize that one approach doesn't work for every client. People absorb information in a variety of ways so you'll need to discover and implement adaptive teaching methods. Although this process may be time consuming, you'll be much more willing to do so if you have an emotional investment in the outcome.

You'll need to remember people are hiring you to help them make progress toward a goal. Once they meet that goal, your services may no longer be needed. Can you find joy in this completion as opposed to being upset about losing income?

You're also in a rare position to get a great deal of feedback about the value you provide. Many professionals have to wait for a monthly, quarterly, or even annual review that is comprised of feedback from just a few people. Of course, this feedback won't all be positive. If you truly enjoy helping people, you'll be able view negative feedback as an opportunity to improve the quality of your work. In the best situations, this feedback is extremely detailed, providing specific guidance on how to further hone your craft. Keep in mind, some people are just miserable, and their negative feedback has nothing to do with you.

One of your greatest rewards will be the gratitude expressed by those you've helped. I often get thank-you emails or LinkedIn messages from people I've worked with 1:1 or have heard me speak at various events. One person—who lives in Austin, Texas—even offered to drive me around on his pedicab when he heard I would be speaking at SXSW!

Later, we'll discuss developing a process for how you'll leverage this positive feedback. Should you ask for a referral? Can you leverage it as a testimonial?

From a less tactical perspective, positive feedback provides much needed recognition for a job well done and the motivation to keep pushing forward through challenging times.

Can You Effectively Pitch and Sell Your Services?

For some people, being a salesperson is a full-time job. As a coach or consultant, it can take up a decent percentage of your time as well. You'll need to clearly develop a process for explaining what you do, who you do it for, why you're the best option, and how you'll close deals. Fortunately, we'll cover all of this in the coming chapters. I understand some of you may be more introverted, which is why we'll also focus on more passive approaches to attracting and even closing your ideal clients. You're eventually going to have to talk to someone, but you can still close deals from your website alone.

One issue that you'll undoubtedly encounter is pricing. Should you charge hourly or by the project? How much should you charge? As a coach or consultant your hourly rate will seem rather high when compared to a W-2 employee. This is because you typically won't work a 40-hour week and don't enjoy the same benefits. Saying you charge $100 per hour for social media coaching may seem high at first, but that price is rather reasonable here in New York City.

Unfortunately, this misunderstanding can often lead to undercharging for your service. When I first started out, my rate was way too low. In fact, one prospect even said "Wow, that's cheap"—definitely not the impression you want to leave with someone! The fee you set says a lot about how much other people should value your services, so charge accordingly. That's not to say you should overcharge in order to be seen as more of a professional. The market will eventually tell you what your rate should be. If you keep losing business due to a high rate, to the extent that you can't hit your revenue goal, something needs to change. You'll either need to adjust your rate or do a better job of reinforcing why you're worth the fee you set. Testimonials and references are a great way to justify your rate, so be sure to have them readily available and visible on your website. Gathering this third-party validation takes time. You'll come to realize the time spent working *on* your business will help you more efficiently work *in* your business.

My goal with this book is to help fast-forward that discovery process. We'll cover how to determine a rate aligned with your revenue goals, and much needed time off.

Can You Leverage Technology and Learn New Skills?

As is the case with any entrepreneur, you'd be surprised how many skills you develop that aren't directly related to your core offering. If you maintain your own website, you might spend a weekend learning the ins and outs of Squarespace. Plan on having a newsletter? You could easily find yourself spending hours watching Mailchimp tutorials.

Keep in mind, the information you discover may become outdated, or another change may cause you to do additional research. Here's an example. Squarespace now offers an email-delivery platform. Do you stay with Mailchimp, or switch to Squarespace email? How hard would it be to import your emails to Squarespace? Does it have the same features? This is a small example of the decisions you'll face on a regular basis. At a larger company, you could rely on another person to handle all of this so you could focus on doing your job. This is all part of your job.

Beyond that, many apps and tools can greatly increase your efficiency. Blocking off a few hours to discover and implement some of them can pay off big time in the long run. For example, I use Acuity to schedule all my meetings. Instead of asking for a prospect or client's availability, I share mine and it's always up-to-date. They see a variety of options, pick a time that works best for them, and we both automatically get a calendar hold. This is much easier than going back and forth before finally nailing down a date and time. With some prospects, you may even lose them in the process. We'll cover a library of other time saving resources in the coming chapters.

Although this adoption of technology isn't a requirement, you'll save yourself a lot of time by doing so. You'll also save money by not hiring someone else to do tasks that you may be able to accomplish.

Have You Considered Your Self-Care Routine?

It's easy to sacrifice a workout when you know just one more email *might* land you a new client. Or, to get caught up in the "hustle harder" way of thinking and ignore your personal relationships.

Don't do it.

Eventually, you'll break down. You can't operate at your best without a self-care routine. Plan your days, weeks, and months with that in mind.

This will be good for your health *and* your business. If you're constantly stressed out from being overworked, it's going to have a negative impact on your personality. If you are a coach or consultant, that can have severe consequences. Most clients want to work with people who are good at their job *and* are genuinely nice to be around. You can't show up as the best version of yourself without a maintenance routine.

The moments you set aside to hit the gym, meditate, or whatever you need to do to take care of yourself will help you yield even greater results than spending that time working.

You'll also need to block off time for vacation. An extended period of rest will leave you recharged and ready to continue building your business. This can be challenging to do as a consultant since you're essentially trading time for money. For this reason, you'll need to adjust your rate accordingly. You have the opportunity to design your business around your life as opposed to designing your life around your business. There's no reason you can't be happy, healthy, and successful.

Understanding Your Audience and the Problems You'll Solve

Starting a consulting business is all about understanding the needs of potential clients and responding to them. Before you jump into starting a consulting business, you first have to think a bit about what you're good at and how it might dovetail with what potential clients need. It's really an awareness exercise—knowing who you are, what you can offer, and how it might be useful to others.

That is why you also need to think about the word *empathy*. You may be an expert in your field, but no one will trust you to solve their problems until you've demonstrated an understanding of them and their associated challenges. I know it's a buzzword that can often be overused, but *empathy* is key to creating a real connection with your audience.

This empathy and understanding allows you to say, "I understand you have this problem. I know the impact it's having on you, and I have a solution to share with you." It also helps you avoid making a very common mistake: building solutions for problems that don't exist or aren't impactful enough for people to pay you a sufficient amount.

In this chapter, you'll learn how to perform audience research at little to no cost by thinking about what you do and who you do it for. However, the insights you gain will be invaluable as they'll help you discover how to make a more genuine connection with your audience and create an irresistible to solution to their problems.

Determining What You Do and Who You Do It For

As a consultant you'll need to project confidence in your ability to understand a client's challenges and create the associated solutions. Clarity is the precursor to confidence. To get started, we'll need to establish clarity on two very important aspects of your consulting business: What you do, and who you do it for. Establishing this clarity is extremely important. If you're unclear on the service you provide, or the audience you provide it to, people won't perceive you as an expert.

I'll give you a real example. When I first launched my consulting company, I decided I would focus only on Facebook and Google Ads. I had just left my full-time role at Facebook, and I previously worked as a Google Ads consultant at Adobe. A few months in, someone asked me if I did Yelp ads as well.

I didn't want to lose the opportunity, and I knew I could teach myself in about a week, so I said yes. Then another person asked me if I could help set up their Google Analytics account. I already knew how to do that, even though I really didn't enjoy it. But I didn't want to lose that opportunity either, so I went along with it.

Here's the problem with that: As my business started to gain momentum, I wasn't the "go-to" guy for any specific service. I was more of a Swiss army knife of digital marketing. Now, Swiss army knives provide value in a pinch, and they're great to have on hand. But let's pretend you own a restaurant and need to open expensive bottles of wine on a regular basis. Sure, you could use the corkscrew that comes with the Swiss army knife, but you're better off getting a real wine bottle opener. You might even pay more for it because it does a better job and is more aligned with what your customers expect. As a consultant, you want to be that high-end wine bottle opener. But to do that, you have to determine and operate in your zone of genius.

In the *The Big Leap: Conquer Your Hidden Fear and Take Life to the Next Level* (HarperOne, 2010), author Gay Hendricks describes the various zones of function. They are as follows:

- ▶ *Zone of Incompetence.* Activities you struggle to accomplish and don't enjoy. For me, that's using advanced functions in Excel. I still can't do a V-Lookup no matter how many YouTube videos I watch.
- ▶ *Zone of Competence.* These are activities that you can perform moderately well, but others can do it just as well, and bring you little to no satisfaction. If you previously worked in-house, these could have been your day-to-day job responsibilities! You may have felt like you were just going through the motions and weren't necessarily expressing your innate capabilities through your work.
- ▶ *Zone of Excellence.* This includes activities in which you excel, for which you're a recognized expert, but don't challenge you intellectually and deliver little to no satisfaction. Again, this could have been something you focused on during your career, but you just had a nagging feeling that you wanted to do more, even if it seemed counterintuitive to those around you. You have to be really careful with this zone. People will be willing to pay you good money for your expertise, but your heart may not be in it. Beyond that, it could be distracting you from operating in the final zone.
- ▶ *Zone of Genius.* These are activities that you excel at and want to keep developing. Time flies and you feel energized when you're engaging in them. They bring personal satisfaction and you're excited to learn more. You may have been able to dabble in this zone from time to time but have been held back for one reason or another. This can lead to frustration, which can lead to you leaving your job so you could pursue more meaningful work. If you were laid off, believe it or not, you may have been given the gift of autonomy, allowing you to further develop this zone even if you weren't quite prepared to do so.

As a consultant, operating in your zone of genius could be something as simple as writing an insightful blog or attending an informative webinar. On the other hand, it could include performing deep research on your industry and summarizing your findings in an eBook or speaking topic.

When people talk about having a growth mindset, this is very much aligned with operating in and further mastering your zone of genius.

On my end, I genuinely love helping people best determine how to monetize their knowledge. It's so amazing to me that you could have this information, that we package into a service, and you then use that to pay your bills and support the lifestyle you desire.

You should be this fired up about the service you offer as well. So, we're going to walk through an exercise that will help you determine your zone of genius. This will eventually help us determine the service you're going to offer.

Now, if you already have a good handle on that, consider this as an opportunity to further refine what you offer.

I should also note, you may have a few zones of genius that you combine to make an even more niche offering. I spoke to a woman who was a user experience expert and also excelled at developing employee benefit programs. We determined that she could offer UX consulting for employee benefit programs. If employees don't know how to use the website, they won't use the benefits, and companies wouldn't reach their desired outcomes from the programs. Super niche, but it's easy to become the go-to person in that area.

So, now let's go through a mind-mapping exercise where we home in on your zone of genius.

Determining Your Zone of Genius

Before we get started, I suggest checking out the spreadsheet that accompanies this activity on my website (terryrice.co/bookresources). This may make it easier to follow along, and you'll be able to immediately implement what you've learned.

You'll start by setting up a spreadsheet that has the four zones listed in columns.

Then, create another column to the right labeled "Roles."

Start by listing all the roles you've had in your career. This can also include companies you've worked at or organizations you belonged or volunteered at. Also, be sure to list any relevant activities that you would consider yourself to be very good at. Maybe you're really good at organizing living spaces even though you've never done that as a job. You could potentially make a living as an interior design consultant for people who live in small apartments.

On my end, my roles would include Adobe, Facebook, an ad agency here in New York, plus a few other roles.

Then, start reflecting on the activities you performed at each role. It may help to take a look at your resume if you have one handy or open up your LinkedIn profile. For each activity, assign it to one of the four zones. It's important to be completely honest with yourself here. I was an associate director of analytics at a big agency, but it was more or less something I was competent at. I didn't particularly enjoy the work, which is why I left after less than a year.

As you go through this exercise you should have a decent number of activities in the incompetence and competence zone and have less in the excellence and genius zones. That's totally fine—this is how it should look. If you're a genius or excellent at too many things, you may need to shift some of them to the competence zone.

Now that you have this list, take a few minutes to reflect on it. Again, you'll want to spend as much time as possible in your zone of genius. That said, it's OK if you spend some time in your zone of excellence, especially if you're a solopreneur—that's just part of the job.

For example, if you're teaching someone how to do Facebook ads, budgeting has to be part of it. It may not be your favorite thing to do in the world, but it's necessary to the success of the project.

When you look at your zones of genius and excellence, it should feel like a natural way to share your knowledge with a defined audience.

Based on my experience before starting my consulting career, I would have landed on the following, as shown in Figure 1–1.

Genius	Excellence
Facebook ads	Budgeting
Explaining complex topics	Google Ads
Campaign strategy	Analyzing data

FIGURE 1–1: **Example of Zones**

Of course, yours will look different, but you're already on your way to defining the service you'll offer.

Defining Your Target Audience

Now that we have an idea of the value you can provide, we need to get specific on the audience you'll provide it for. Typically, the more specific, the better. Most of you have heard the phrase, the riches are in the niches, and it's often true.

Let's say you're a nonprofit looking to leverage email marketing, and you want to work with someone who's an expert at using email to activate donors. You may come across someone who's a great overall email marketer, but they may not understand the nuances of getting people to make a donation as opposed to completing a purchase.

Being more specific is great for you because it allows you to go deeper in your zone of genius.

You'll essentially be able to say, *"I only do this for this specific audience, and I'm going to continue enhancing my expertise because I'm excited about it."*

Again, this is something that I messed up with in the beginning. My background was primarily in business-to-consumer (B2C) offerings, and I was really good at helping companies selling consumer products. But, once I went independent, I started working with several different industries: Nonprofits, hospitality, travel and even some finance. I'd say I was at least competent in most of them, but it wasn't something I was passionate about.

If you don't have experience working with various audiences, it's OK to explore the options available. It's hard to fully understand what you enjoy if you haven't had some not-so-pleasant experiences. But over time, you'll want to narrow down your scope so you have more clarity around what you do and how you present yourself.

Either way we're about to walk through an exercise that will help you initially home in on the audience you want to serve.

Determining Your Target Audience

Again, you're going to open up a spreadsheet and you'll find a template on my website terryrice.co/bookresources.

Start listing all the audiences you could service in the first column. Based on your service, this could run the gamut, but try to stay somewhat within the constraints of what you offer. So, if you offer Salesforce integration consulting, "business-to-business (B2B) organizations" would be a good fit, but you wouldn't list "stay-at-home dads." I'll provide some examples to get you started.

- ► Nonprofits
- ► Retail
- ► Business-to-business (B2B)
- ► Business-to-consumer (B2C)
- ► Stay-at-home dads
- ► Finance

▶ Travel

▶ Auto

▶ Graduating seniors

▶ Medical

▶ Agencies

▶ Retail

▶ Pet owners

▶ Restaurants

▶ Frequent travelers

▶ Education

▶ ecommerce

The number of audiences you come up with will vary based on service offering, but you should at least have two or three. This will help you make sure you're at least considering other audiences, even if you're pretty sure where you want to focus.

Now, take some time to reflect on your list. Which of these audiences do you definitely not want to work with? It's usually easier to reduce the available options and then sift through what's left.

For me, that would be auto, finance, medical, and travel. I try to stay away from regulated industries, and some of these are just way too complicated. You can cross these out or maybe color-code them as red.

Based on my passions and interests, here's where I would land (see Figure 1–2).

Audiences
B2C
Ecommerce
Agencies

FIGURE 1–2: **Potential Audiences**

So, looking at this, I'm landing on ecommerce, B2C, and agencies. Ecommerce can be a subset of B2C in some cases, and I'd enjoy consulting agencies who work with ecommerce or B2C clients.

If we combine this with the other sheet we created, we can start to home in on the service you want to offer (see Figure 1–3 on page 8).

Genius	Excellence	Audience
Facebook ads	Budgeting	B2C
Explaining complex topics	Google Ads	Ecommerce
Campaign strategy	Analyzing data	Agencies

FIGURE 1–3: **Narrowing Down Service Offering**

So now we have your zones of genius and excellence and your audience all lined up. On the left, we have what you do; on the right, you have who you do it for.

This should start to feel like a solid idea. It doesn't have to be perfect, but you're making good progress.

Next step, let's start doing research on our audience so we can best determine how to help, starting with creating the empathy map you read about at the top of the chapter.

Use an Empathy Map

Before you even start envisioning what your consulting business will look like or writing your business plan, you'll need to create an empathy map. Similar to a user persona, an empathy map goes deeper into the psychographics of your target audience. These are commonly used by UX professionals as a step in design thinking, but they can be leveraged in other sectors as well. With empathy maps, you can gain a more complete understanding of your audience, and reflect that in the consulting services you offer and how you communicate the value provided. Although you'll have several people in this audience, you'll want to construct this as if you're referring to one person. Early on, choose an avatar that represents your ideal client. An avatar is a representation of your ideal customer—the type of person you want to work with and their associated characteristics. Keep in mind, you may have more than one, but focus on the most impactful at the outset. Use empathy to prove you understand them and what they'd like to accomplish, then position your consulting service as a solution.

Creating this map will take a fair amount of effort. This is what I refer to as the "lonely work." Nobody sees it, and you won't see any immediate impact. You may be tempted to phone it in and just get started. Don't. This is when you separate yourself from everyone who is trying to take the easy way out and offering their services without laying the groundwork to understand their prospective clients. This is where you commit to excellence and master the game within the game.

An empathy map consists of six sections that highlight what's going on in your target audience's head. You can see an example in Figure 1–4.

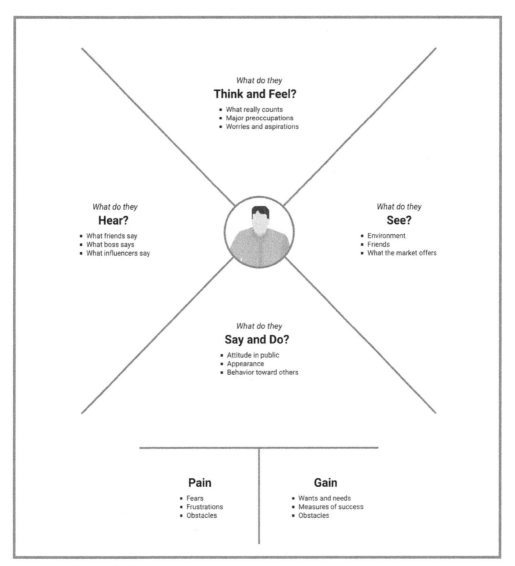

FIGURE 1–4: **Empathy Map**

Every consultant's empathy map will look different depending on the industry they work in. For example, let's say you're a digital marketing consultant who works with ecommerce brands. Here is what the elements of the empathy map you create for potential clients would look like:

Think and Feel:

- ▶ I can't bring in more inventory until I sell through what I have.
- ▶ I'm glad I have control over my own destiny.
- ▶ I think I can figure out how to run ads myself, but there's just so much information out there.
- ▶ SEO is confusing and expensive.

Hear:

- ▶ You have to focus on Instagram to get sales.
- ▶ Optimize your site for mobile.
- ▶ Content marketing is a must.
- ▶ Hustle harder!

See:

- ▶ Other brands have way more followers.
- ▶ Positive feedback from customers.
- ▶ Our sales are down 20 percent.
- ▶ The website could use some tweaks.

Say and Do:

- ▶ Read blogs and watch YouTube videos.
- ▶ Meet with agencies and freelancers.
- ▶ Attend workshops.
- ▶ I have no clue how much I should budget.

Pain:

- ▶ Agencies and freelancers who make promises with no proof.

Gain:

- ▶ No long-term contracts.

Knowing this about your target audience gives you valuable input in regard to the services you offer and how you communicate with your audience. I'll reference this several times in upcoming chapters.

Build the Empathy Map

Your empathy map will be one of the most powerful tools you have as you start your consulting business, but it takes time to develop. Beyond that, you'll continually make updates as you learn more about your audience or environmental changes occur. For example, in the case of a digital marketing consultant, a new social media platform emerging could easily warrant updating your map.

The following approaches will help you build and refine your map over time.

Attend Workshops Related to Your Area of Expertise

When I first launched my company, I attended as many free in-person events as possible. The New York City Small Business Services routinely offers classes to the public at no charge. I would attend to better understand my audience and determine what information was readily available for free. Since I was obviously going to charge for my service, it definitely had to be better, or at least more bespoke. After attending several events, I noticed patterns in the questions and concerns expressed by the attendees. Although I hadn't planned on it at the time, I was gaining valuable information that would eventually be included in my empathy map. It's important to note that this information has to come from a large number of individuals. Just because one person said something one time doesn't mean it reflects your audience as a whole. Your goal is to find clusters of themes that you have observed on several occasions. Another benefit of attending these events is the ability to chat with attendees in real time. Ask attendees why they started their business, how things are going, what surprises them, etc. Be upfront about your background, but make it clear that your consulting business isn't operational yet. Since you aren't selling anything, it can be easier to have a casual and genuine conversation. You'll know you are onto something when people start giving you their business cards and asking how you can help them!

I have had good success with making possible client connections when attending industry events and workshops. This was extremely low pressure for me since I wasn't operational, but it got me comfortable chatting with my audience and making some connections in the area.

Attend Meetups Aligned with Your Target Audience

This is similar to the approach above, but the content and structure of these events may differ. For example, when I was building my consulting business, I would attend Meetups for business owners in the Brooklyn area. The attendees weren't necessarily there to talk about digital marketing (which is what I primarily consulted on back then), but I'd learn about other aspects of their business and their overall personality. You can do the same to find out more about your local client base.

Your empathy map needs to reflect all aspects of your audience, not just information directly related to the service you offer. You'll miss a lot by being self-centered. By attending these Meetups, you can discover other areas of concern, including the rising cost of real estate, securing small business loans, and the challenges of maintaining a work-life balance.

None of this information made me a better digital marketer, but it was easier to relate with potential clients on a personal level. Ultimately, people want to work with individuals who are good at their job *and* who they actually enjoy chatting with.

One of my buddies, a financial advisor, took a similar approach. She attended free events that catered to high-net-worth individuals, even though she wasn't even close to having a high net worth. Again, her goal was to be a fly on the wall. She learned about the types of investments these individuals made, including art and watches, which helped her better understand how to position the portfolio she offered. She also discovered what they did in their free time. For example, they were much more likely to attend a show at the Brooklyn Academy of Music as opposed to catching a Brooklyn Nets game at Barclays Center. Once she officially launched her business, she came to realize how powerful simply referencing relevant art and cultural events was to creating a bond with potential clients. These people get pitched all the time; they want someone who truly gets them.

tip

Emotional IQ is one of the defining characteristics of a good consultant, and the importance will only continue to increase as more tasks become automated. As you build your empathy map and learn about your possible clients, you are practicing emotional IQ.

Attend Relevant Conferences and Events That Charge a Fee

The main benefit of attending events that charge a fee is that you know you're among people who are willing to part with money in exchange for information.

I've attended and led discussions at several free events. In regard to attendees, there's often a stark contrast. I'm not saying the information gathered from free events isn't useful, but it's beneficial to supplement your findings with an audience of individuals who pay to attend events. Beyond being willing to part with money, they're often more high-intent prospects. Individuals who attend free events are more likely to be casually interested in a topic as opposed to people who attend paid events.

Since you're paying to attend as well, choose wisely. If you're on a tight budget, you may have to skip this option for now or find a way to attend without paying. I've often volunteered to work at events in exchange for a free ticket. Consider reaching out to see if the event organizer needs ushers, someone to set up rooms, etc. You'll notice some events actively solicit volunteers on their website.

For example, I was able to score a free ticket to Social Media Week by providing editorial coverage of events. My coverage was posted on their website, which gave me an additional way to reach potential clients. A year later, I delivered a keynote at the same event. That's a side benefit of connecting with event organizers—you can start a relationship that may blossom over time.

Perform Social Listening on Reddit and Similar Channels

This is a great option for people who can't get out too often, or live in an area that doesn't offer as many in-person events. Social listening involves tracking, analyzing, and responding to conversations about your brand and industry online. It's a key component of audience research. Since you're just now building your brand, you'll be focused on learning more about your target audience.

Reddit is often a great source of information since it's so easy to find extremely specific communities comprising of individuals who share their thoughts and experiences with others. Anyone can post and respond. If users like a post, they'll give it an Upvote. An Upvote is how users can signal their approval or support for a post. Upvotes move a post toward the top of the site. Look for posts that have a lot of Upvotes and a decent number of comments. This will show you what is truly resonating with your audience.

For example, I met Soda Kuczkowski, a sleep health educator and founder of Start With Sleep, during a class I was teaching at General Assembly, a school that helps individuals develop the skills of tomorrow. Along with being a credentialed expert in her field, she regularly visits the r/insomnia Reddit community to learn more about and interact with her audience. You can see an example of what a Reddit exchange looks like in Figure 1–5 on page 14.

This is how she discovered and was reminded of some of the frustrations voiced by her audience, such as family members telling them to try going to bed earlier or put lavender on their pillow. Knowing what remedies her audience has already tried helped further position herself as an expert while expressing empathy at the same time.

Here's an example of the content that could be developed based on these insights:

I know you've already tried some of the common remedies, such as putting lavender on your pillow. These are all great suggestions, but sometimes it just won't cut it, that's where I come in.

Simply acknowledging their frustration is the first step in creating a genuine bond.

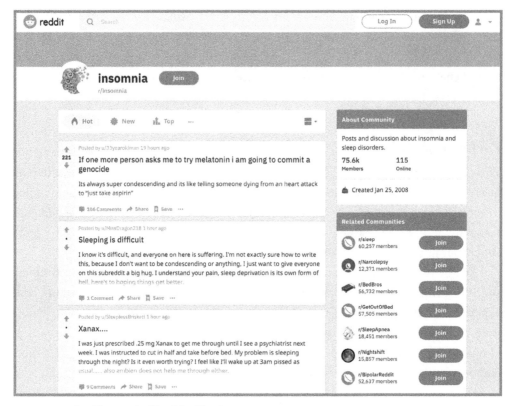

FIGURE 1–5: **An Example Reddit Exchange**

Twitter is another platform you should consider monitoring, even if you don't plan on posting content. In this case, you'll follow hashtags that are relevant to your audience. Sticking with the same example, #insomnia proved to be a gold mine of information for my sleep consultant friend. By following these posts, she was able to get a better idea of what their audience was discussing around the topic of insomnia. They were also much more likely to review sleeping aids and remedies on this platform. You can see an example in Figure 1–6 on page 15.

Following insomnia-related hashtags on Instagram provided similar results and also helped her discover how other sleep consultants were engaging with the audience. This engagement was often a brand-building exercise, which I will discuss later in Chapter 10 when we take a deep dive into marketing.

tip

Consider posting in relevant Reddit and Facebook communities. To increase your response rate, keep it anonymous, or at least offer that as an option.

FIGURE 1–6: **An Example Twitter Exchange**

Interview People Who Are in Your Target Audience

A real-time conversation is clearly one of the best ways to learn more about the audience you'll serve. You can ask open-ended questions and encourage them to elaborate on specific responses. Do your best not to ask leading questions or express your personal opinion so you don't influence their responses.

If you already know people in your target audience, you can invite them to connect in person or via phone. Be respectful of their time, and send over a list of questions you have so they can be more prepared. I suggest recording the interview, if possible. You'll be able to maintain eye contact and won't miss any important details. You can use a program like Descript (www.descript.com) to transcribe the audio file to text.

For those prospects with whom you are only loosely associated or are often short on time, consider doing the interview via email. Of course, an obvious barrier to success with this method is finding people who will chat with you. Email interviews are a great option in this situation as well. Better yet, set up a Google form so you can send a link as opposed to an email. Beyond that, you'll be able to easily aggregate and export the responses.

Here are some questions to consider asking of prospective clients:

▶ What is the most difficult hurdle you are dealing with on a daily basis when it comes to running an ecommerce business?

▶ What's blocking you right now from overcoming that hurdle?

▶ In regard to overcoming this hurdle, what have you already tried?

▶ Where do you normally find information about this topic?

▶ What would life look like after you overcame that hurdle? How would your personal and professional life be better?

▶ If you had a magic wand and could create the perfect solution to overcome that hurdle, what would it be?

▶ If someone offered a strategy to create this perfect solution for you, what would you be willing to pay for it?

▶ Is there anything else you would like to add?

Of course, these questions will vary based on your expertise. If at all possible, talk to people who have previously paid to get help resolving their challenges. This is the audience you'll eventually work with.

Once you have the responses, sort them by question and length. Often, longer responses will provide you with more beneficial information. This approach will also be helpful if you have a large number of responses. Ideally, you want to aim for around 60 to 70 responses, but that's not always possible.

Now that you've compiled all this information, you can populate your empathy map. Once complete, share your map with select people in your target audience, ask how well it reflects who they are, and make adjustments as needed.

Keep in mind, this is a living document and will most likely change over time—and you may have more than one empathy map if you serve multiple kinds of clients. That's a good thing; it shows your understanding of your audience is evolving and reflects any changes in their environment as well.

You can download a template for your empathy map on my website (www.terryrice. co/bookresources).

Determining the Problems You'll Solve

Once you've developed your empathy map, you'll leverage it to determine the specific problems you'll solve for your consulting clients.

Problems
Unable to determine budget
Not sure how to track results
Website functionality
Not even sure where to start
Unclear on how to target FB/IG audience
Optimizing campaigns
Hiring freelance/employees
Email integration
Not sure how to write ad copy/what to say
Need videos/high-quality photos
Uneasy about running ads
Don't know what a good cost per conversion is

FIGURE 1–7: **Example Problems Column**

Review the content from your empathy map, and identify information that reflects a specific problem your audience has. Now, leverage the worksheet provided, and enter this information in the column labeled "Problems."

We'll stick with the digital marketing consultant for this example in Figure 1–7.

You most likely won't be able to, or want to, solve every problem your target audience has. That's fine. Even being aware of these problems will make you a better business partner. For your services, identify problems you can solve and note the associated solution. It's fine if some problems have the same solution. See Figure 1–8 on page 18.

Next, if possible, group these solutions in a sequential manner. What step would come first, second, etc.? In this case, campaign planning would be a logical place to start, and it would make sense to end with optimization. See Figure 1–9 on page 18.

You can always revise what you've come up with; the goal here is to get something documented as a starting point.

Why This Is Important

The goal of this chapter is to gain a deeper, unbiased understanding of your target audience. This will allow you to develop and express the value of solutions you have to their specific problems.

Problems	Solution
Unable to determine budget	Campaign planning
Not sure how to track results	Measurement
Website functionality	
Not even sure where to start	Campaign planning
Unclear on how to target FB/IG audience	Campaign tactics
Optimizing campaigns	Optimization
Hiring freelance/employees	
Email integration	
Not sure how to write ad copy/what to say	Campaign tactics
Need videos/high-quality photos	
Uneasy about running ads	Execution
Don't know what a good cost per conversion is	Key performance indicators

FIGURE 1–8: **Sample Problems and Solutions**

Problems	Solution	Service
Unable to determine budget	Campaign planning	Campaign planning
Not sure how to track results	Measurement	Key performance indicators
Website functionality		Campaign tactics
Not even sure where to start	Campaign planning	Execution
Unclear on how to target FB/IG audience	Campaign tactics	Measurement
Optimizing campaigns	Optimization	Optimization
Hiring freelance/employees		
Email integration		
Not sure how to write ad copy/what to say	Campaign tactics	
Need videos/high-quality photos		
Uneasy about running ads	Execution	
Don't know what a good cost per conversion is	Key performance indicators	

FIGURE 1–9: **Putting It All Together**

As your business continues to evolve, you'll be able to attract and win business just by putting in the extra effort to look at problems from your audience's point of view.

Action Items

▶ Review the empathy map guide provided by the Nielsen Norman Group (https://www.nngroup.com/articles/empathy-mapping/).

▶ Research relevant free or low-cost local events to attend. Don't plan on pitching or selling; just engage with and learn about your audience.

▶ Perform social listening by monitoring relevant channels and hashtags.

▶ Create your empathy map and revisit it every six months. Make adjustments as needed.

▶ Document the problems you'll solve and the associated solutions.

▶ Complete the following fields in The One Page Business Plan: Target Client, Client Problems, Solutions Wanted

CHAPTER

2

Business Models, Pricing, and Goal Setting

Although you may want to charge in and start looking for your first clients right away, you'll need to start by setting up measurable and attainable goals. For a consultant, that means that you will want to view those goals through the lens of how you set up your business and how you set your prices. This chapter will discuss how to map out your initial business plan on a quarterly, monthly, weekly, and daily basis. Then, I will walk you through the basics you need to know about how to set fair and profitable pricing structures.

In fact, how you determine your pricing structure is directly tied to the goals you set. Consultants often ask me how much they should charge for their services. It all starts with a goal; you have to determine how much money you would like to make. Setting a yearly amount can be incredibly challenging when you're first starting out. Sure, you may want to make $100,000 a year, but is it reasonable? While it makes sense to start with an annual goal, you'll want to evaluate on a monthly basis and consider making adjustments on a quarterly basis.

But to get there, you first have to map out actual plans to achieve your goals. Initially, you may spend more time working *on* your business as opposed to working *in* your business. Working *on* your business includes activities such as creating content, setting up business processes, and prospecting. Working *in* your business is actively doing work that generates revenue. Because of this, it can be challenging to determine the impact of working on your business until you start signing clients. The best way to get started on setting your goals is to think about what kind of consulting model you want to use.

Choose a Business Model

Before you can sign those clients and make that goal amount you've set for yourself, you'll need to determine your business model. In short, a business model is how you plan to make money. As a consultant, you have a number of options. I'll explain these while also discussing the pros and cons of each kind of model. Let's start there.

Time-Based Model

The time-based model is pretty common and straightforward. In this model, your rate and scope of work are determined at the outset. You can choose to have an hourly rate or a day rate. Your rate is determined by "the market" and how you present yourself vs. the competition. Notice, I didn't say "how experienced" you are vs. the competition, as that is a different metric altogether. In any model, presentation has a lot to do with how you'll be rewarded, and we'll get into that more during Chapter 6.

The benefit of this model is that as a consultant, you are paid for each hour of actual work. It can sometimes be challenging to scope the amount of time it will take to address your client's needs; this model protects you from underbidding. However, this also requires detailed record keeping. For example, when I worked at Adobe, we had to document every

15 minutes of billable work. This could easily take two to three hours per week, which wasn't billable to the client. Beyond that, clients may ask why something took so long. You may end up explaining why you had to research one thing or another before coming to a conclusion, which eats up even more of your time.

tip

Be upfront with your clients about how you bill in a time-based model, and set expectations for what will happen if a project goes over the projected time frame.

Natalie Allport is the founder of 93 Agency (www.93agency.com), a social media marketing and consulting agency. She shares her experience with business models: "At first I charged hourly, but being an ongoing service that I offer, I realized that monthly packages would serve me best. After about six months of hourly, as I improved at my deliverables, and was delivering the same results but for less time, I realized that monthly packages would work best not just for selling service offerings, but also for predicting cash flow and managing internal operations."

Like Natalie, your model may evolve over time as well.

Project-Based Model

With a project-based model, you agree to perform a specific type of work for a predetermined amount of money. Before starting, the details of all deliverables will be agreed upon by both parties.

An advantage of this approach is that consultants can focus on providing value as opposed to watching a clock. You'll also have more predictable income since that revenue is more or less locked in once the contract is signed. Once you have enough projects signed, you can back off prospecting and lead generation, to an extent. I'm not saying you should completely stop looking for new business, but you won't have the same sense of urgency. Beyond that, experienced professionals who can get the job done quicker are rewarded, without having to bill several hours to earn their fee. This doesn't mean you're rushing to complete a project. You can just get the job done faster because you've already learned some tactics or techniques in the past that can move things along faster. Remember: You're paid on the value you provide, not how long it took you to do it.

One of the drawbacks of this model is underestimating the amount of time it will take to complete a project. Back when I focused on digital marketing, I had some projects take twice as long as they should have because people couldn't figure out how to log in to their Facebook account, or their Google Analytics data wasn't formatted properly. You'll likely encounter similar situations. Initially, it can be challenging to scope how long a project will take. These are the growing pains associated with consulting. Over time, and with experience, you'll be able to estimate timing based on previous engagements.

Another drawback is "scope creep." This is when a client intentionally or unintentionally keeps adding more tasks that weren't outlined in the original contract. This happened frequently with another digital marketing consultant I worked with. A client would ask her to manage their Instagram campaigns, and then ask her to create the content as well. This extra work easily tripled the amount of time she was spending (which included numerous creative revisions), but the client was unwilling to pay her more for it. Eventually, she walked away from the opportunity. Days later, they emailed her back and paid her the amount she had requested.

Again, over time, you'll get better at protecting yourself from this by creating more detailed contracts. When scope creep does come up, just inform your client this would be an extra line item that comes with additional charges.

Retainer-Based Model

This model involves providing ongoing or as-needed service over a set period of time. Unlike the project-based model, this model doesn't necessarily involve a specific deliverable. Instead, it allows you and the client to agree on a set, recurring price and provides flexibility in the scope of the work and deliverables you provide.

I often work on a retainer model for clients who want to have access to me in case anything comes up. For example, this might be a smart model if you are working on a particularly challenging business opportunity, or a client needs a second set of eyes on a proposal. I've also received calls and texts that need an immediate answer. I'm happy to be that go-to resource, and a retainer-based model allows me to be that person for my clients.

For the client, a retainer model is almost like a safety net. At any given moment, they know there's a knowledge resource available who already has background information on their company.

For consultants, retainers provide a predictable source of income, which may be passive during slower periods. This allows you to focus more on business development and other areas of interest in your consulting business. One drawback is not being able to charge as much as you would for a defined project. Beyond that, you'll still have to keep an eye out for scope creep and make adjustments as needed. Keep in mind, scope creep can also be an aspect of how often and when a client expects you to communicate. Sure, you're more or less "on call" if they need you, but that doesn't mean you're available 24/7. If you originally state you're available from 9 A.M. to 5 P.M. Monday through Friday, and the client starts expecting response outside of that window, you'll need to address this as scope creep.

tip

Establish a service-level agreement (SLA) in regard to how quickly you'll respond to requests and your service hours.

In a utopian situation, you'll be able to lock in a long-term retainer model with a client you genuinely enjoy working with.

Results-Based Model

In this model, you're compensated based on the results the client achieves. Typically, this means that you are paid a percentage of profits or money saved.

For example:

▶ A business development consultant may charge a percentage of new business their work generates.

▶ A technology optimization consultant may charge a percentage of the money saved based on their recommendations.

The benefit of this model is that you are paid in direct proportion to the value you create. This is attractive to the client as it reduces their overall risk, and you can often get a higher fee as a result. If things go well, you can make a great deal of revenue, especially if you implement processes that don't need to be actively maintained.

The downside is that you could do an amazing job, and the results could still be dismal. When I worked as a digital marketing consultant, I was often contacted for results-based work. I could send traffic to a website, but if the UX was bad, or if the products were subpar, I wasn't going to make any money. So, it's a risk that you take as a consultant. There are several factors that go into determining whether or not it's worth the risk:

▶ Will you still be able to support yourself, even if you don't generate any money from this project?

▶ How big is the payoff if it's successful?

▶ Is this distracting you from other projects that could be more worthwhile?

You also need to clearly determine how your work will be attributed to any success. Otherwise, you run the risk of not getting credit for a job well done.

Consulting Firm Model

Another option is to go with a consulting firm model. In this situation, you hire freelancers or employees to complete work on your behalf. You still own the relationship with the client, but you have a team that handles some or all of the work.

Anna Vatuone, a personal branding strategist, helps entrepreneurs and executives build their brands. To properly achieve this goal, many of her clients need a website built for them. Anna initially provided this service as well before hiring a vetted freelancer to complete this process. Although she still drives the strategy and content creation, she can leave the nuts and bolts work to a trusted professional. This allows her to spend more one-on-one time with her clients while still meeting their needs.

The consulting firm model gives you a great deal of leverage. You can charge a client $2,000 for a project, then pay a team member $1,000 to complete it. This model also allows you to expand the scope of your offering—especially to tasks that may not be in your own personal wheelhouse.

The downside is that you need to make sure you're still profitable after paying your employees or freelancers to whom you've outsourced work. For example, imagine an unexpected hiccup occurs and the team member you were going to pay $1,000 to complete that task now needs $1,500? You'll need to be highly skilled at project management to avoid these fiascos.

Beyond that, your reputation is on the line so you want to make sure that anyone representing you delivers on your promises. It can be challenging not to micromanage, which can have a negative impact on morale. If you became an independent consultant to avoid the challenges associated with managing others, this may not be the right option for you.

These challenges can include:

▶ Double-checking their work
▶ Dealing with negative feedback about the quality of their work
▶ Navigating any personal issues that may arise
▶ Adjusting their pay or benefits to stay competitive with other employment opportunities

You may have an amazing experience managing and nurturing your team, but it's important to weigh all aspects involved.

Subcontractor Model

This model involves subcontracting your services to another organization, who takes care of all the sales and billing. You provide the services and receive a set fee from that organization.

This is the model I largely depended on when I first started my company. I led digital marketing training engagements on behalf of the educational organization General Assembly. This was a great way to keep me in front of larger clients including Walmart, Calvin Klein, and Verizon without the risks that went along with running my own company. This model worked very well for me due to the high amount of repeat business I received. Plus, it gave me the opportunity to name drop during prospecting calls. Saying, "I just got back from teaching Walmart the same thing . . ." is a great way to increase your credibility.

Here's the downside: It was almost impossible for me to increase my rates. Although I was fairly compensated, General Assembly had a lot of overhead to cover, which limited their flexibility in how much they could pay me. I knew the amount I received was a percentage of what they billed the client. Outside of that, I wasn't building anything. These weren't my clients; I couldn't directly solicit them for repeat business or ask for testimonials. However, you can still get a testimonial from the company that is working with you as a subcontractor. And, if you continue to do a good job, they'll keep looping you in on other projects.

Even with the inherent limitations, I still recommend aligning with similar opportunities. It's a great way to supplement the income from your own practice, while avoiding the prospecting and sales aspect.

Determining Your Pricing

When I first started my business, I didn't have a good grasp on how much to charge. Like many new independent consultants, I just wanted to get that first "yes" from a client. Over time, my mindset shifted. I discovered I wasn't charging a fee; my clients were making an investment. This simple shift in thinking made all the difference in how I valued my time and how confidently I presented myself. So long as the value I provided gave good returns on the investment my clients made, we would all be happy in the end.

So, how do you get to a place where you feel like you can charge what you're worth? And how do you communicate that to prospective clients? You have to speak the clients' language, and that means showing them the value of your services. But this is the problem: many consultants don't focus on return on investment (ROI) to justify their fees; they talk about their experience and magical proprietary process. To win business, you need to focus on what you'll do for the prospect. You need to show them value.

This sentiment is echoed in a report by The Predictive Index (www.predictiveindex.com/), which surveyed 152 consultants from firms of all sizes. Rabih Shanshiry, vice president of partner success for The Predictive Index, said, "To be successful, our partner consultants find that grounding proposals with measurable outcomes ensures clients feel confident they will see return on investment (ROI)—which increases growth and retention."

This same report cited, "The ROI of a consultant is too hard to measure" as the main reason why some companies choose not to hire consulting services.

Let's start determining your pricing structure by walking through how you can charge for the value you provide, no matter what business model you use. To illustrate the thinking process behind determining pricing, let's look at a conversation I had with a prospective client, Lorie, who wanted to ramp up her speaking schedule. Lorie is an experienced professional who just started consulting and would like to launch a paid speaking career as well. In this conversation, I was working with her to determine pricing for my services. For the sake of brevity, I'll provide a streamlined version of this conversation:

Terry: What are your goals in regard to speaking? How often would you like to speak?

Lorie: I'm not looking to pay all my bills with it, but I believe it could be a good source of income. Outside of that, I know it's a great way to get in front of my audience and land more clients.

Terry: Got it, thanks. So, as a relatively new speaker, you can expect to earn up to $2,500 per speech, and you want to speak about once a month. To be conservative, let's say you're going to get $1,500 per speech and you do this ten times per year instead of 12. Besides, it's going to take a few months to ramp up anyway. That would net out to $15,000 in your first year. Would that be acceptable?

Lorie: Sure, that sounds good. I imagine I can make even more than that as a result of the prospecting opportunities.

Terry: I'm sure you can too, but let's stick with something that's a bit easier to measure for now. The accelerator program I offer requires a $5,000 investment. If we meet this goal, which we've both agreed is rather conservative, you'll earn $15,000 in revenue and get a 200 percent ROI. Beyond that, you stated you want to continue doing this for the next several years. Even if you never increase your rate and only speak ten times per year, your ROI will be 800 percent after three years. Does that sound good to you?

In this situation, I downplayed the impact of working with me by design and I was rather overt about it. I'd much rather underpromise and overdeliver as opposed to the other way around. I'm not saying you should sell yourself short. It's OK to acknowledge best-case scenarios, but people can tell when you're trying to sell them something that you may not be able to deliver on. That's a horrible way to start a relationship, and may very well be the end of it. That's why I tempered expectations with Lori.

You need to get as close as possible to identifying the return from working with you. If you're working with an individual, aim for at least 200 percent ROI. Again, this means if they pay you $5,000, they will make an incremental $15,000 in revenue. You can see an example in Figure 2–1.

Average fee per speaking engagement	$1,500
Speaking events per year	10
Revenue generated from speaking events	$15,000
Cost of accelerator program	$5,000
ROI (revenue – cost)/revenue	200%

FIGURE 2–1: **ROI from an Accelerator Program**

When working with a corporation, aim for 500 percent or more. They should already have team members who can help them attain marginal increases; you're there to make a larger impact. This will be a bit trickier to calculate due to the numerous variable involved. For example:

▶ How many people are on their team?
▶ How much work needs to be done?
▶ Do they need to bring in additional outside help?
▶ How competitive is the market?

Depending on the services provided, you'll typically want to aim for at least a 10 to 15 percent improvement on one of the following:

▶ Conversion rate
▶ Margins
▶ Volume
▶ Revenue
▶ Turnover

For example, if you help corporations reduce their turnover, you would ask them to estimate how much that costs per year in terms of lost productivity and the cost associated with acquiring and training new employees. As time goes by, you'll continue to get better at asking more probing questions for your specific line of business. When you're just starting out, think to yourself, "What questions could I ask to help me better understand what's stopping them from making or saving money?"

In some cases, the benefit won't be financial. The more precisely you can identify the outcomes associated with your service offering, the more justifiable the investment.

When setting price, you'll also want to touch on the opportunity cost involved with doing nothing. In other words, how much money could they lose or waste if they do nothing to address their problem. Instead of asking how much the potential client could gain, ask how much more they have to lose if they continue with the status quo. Going back to Lorie, she can lose $45,000 in incremental revenue over the course of three years on top of an amazing opportunity to grow her brand if she chooses not to use my services.

Back to the (hopefully) million-dollar question: How do you determine your fees? There are three fundamental ways to arrive at this number. Let's explore each one.

Look at the Competitive Landscape

Some competitors or similar companies may overtly state how much they charge for various packages or their hourly rate. I suggest doing some research into your competition to see if you can mine some valuable insights. Remember, these other consultants don't have to offer the exact same service in order to provide a good frame of reference. You'll have an idea of how much prospective clients are willing to invest in outside help.

For example, you may help companies implement a content management system (CMS). They may be willing to pay you the same amount paid to a consultant who helps them set up the HR management solution.

Or, if you offer digital marketing consulting, you could compare your rates to another expert who offers help with public relations.

If you offer a local service, you'll want to see what people are charging in your area. The rates charged in New York City would seem astronomical when compared to what someone would be willing to pay in a smaller metro area like Des Moines.

If you serve a larger market, some of your competitors may be advertising their services on platforms such as Upwork or Fiverr. These are marketplaces for freelancers and clients to connect. You can easily see how much competitors charge on these platforms, but be aware of where they're located. The cost of living varies greatly from region to region, but you have local bills to pay. These platforms may or not feature experts in your line of business, but it's worth taking a look.

During the COVID shutdown, many businesses began to realize how capable they were of working with remote teams. As a result, the value of working with local experts has been diminished.

Ask People Who Have Hired Similar Consultants

This is where the power of your network comes in handy. You're not asking for business; you're just asking for input from those who have hired consultants offering similar services as yours so you can get a ballpark figure for how you could price your services. If you're a member of a relevant social media group, this is a good place to ask that question. You can do so at an in-person event for your chamber of commerce or similar organization. Again, if you offer a local service, ask within your region. As a bonus, ask what made them feel comfortable signing a deal with this other consultant. You may pick up on some valuable tips that will help you craft your own pitch.

Ask Competitors or Individuals Who Offer a Similar Service

This one sounds counterintuitive. Why would a competitor help you build your business? You'd be surprised. First of all, there's enough business to go around. Second, by nature, consultants like helping people. If you belong to a local professional organization, this is a great place to ask fellow consultants what they charge. The relationships you've started will go a long way in regard to people wanting to share with you.

However, if you're doing cold outreach to someone who offers the exact same service as you, I suggest contacting people who live in a different region. Why? Because you don't want them to view your relationship as purely transactional. Again, you'd be surprised how many people are willing to help. A quick search for a relevant job title on LinkedIn will get you started.

tip

Offer some sort of value when asking for someone else's time. Even a $10 Starbucks gift card can increase the number of responses you get.

Ask Potential Prospects

"What's your budget?" is one of the scariest questions you can ask a prospect, but it's often necessary. The more input you can get from actual prospects, the better. Again, this is where your network comes in handy. Have a candid conversation, but make it clear you're not selling anything . . . yet. The chat could go something like this:

Hey, Bill. I'm launching a new consulting business next month and I was wondering if you could help me out with one critical aspect—how much to charge. I'm not trying to sell you anything right now, but I'd love to get your input. Here's the service I'm offering . . . Based on your experience and needs, how much would you be willing to pay for something like this? What would I need to do for you to pay even more?

This is a great way to get candid input, and Bill could easily turn into a client. The last question *"What would I need to do for you pay even more?"* is a great way to refine and expand your offer, as long as it's something you're willing to do.

Finalizing Your Price

In any case, the number you decide to charge will change over time. Too many people saying "yes" could mean you're not charging enough. Too many people saying "no" could mean your price is too high, or maybe it's the way you're presenting yourself. But you need to determine what percentage is "too many."

Mike Swigunkski, founder at Global Career (www.globalcareer.io), helps people jumpstart their remote lives. He says his pricing is based on competition and plans to keep increasing until his close rates drop below 30 percent. Close rate is the percent of people you sign a deal with divided by the total number of deals you're currently working. So, if you get two clients out of five deals you're working, your close rate is 40 percent. Like Mike, you should aim for a close rate of 30 percent or higher.

When determining her rates, Natalie Allport took a three-step approach. "My rates were based off industry averages, an assessment of my own business goals, and the rates I would need to reach those. I also factored in the amount of time and money I would save and/or bring in to a new client." As some of her pricing is based on ROI, it's imperative that she ask probing questions during the project -scoping process.

Amina AlTai, a holistic business and mindset coach (www.aminaaltai.com), considers both the ROI for her clients as well as the overall amount of effort that goes into creating her offering. Amina states, "I used a formula to value my thought-leadership and curriculum. I look at what it cost me to develop, package, market, and deliver. I also look at value-add considerations and then come up with the investment." This is important to keep in mind if you're spending a significant amount of time or money to develop and deliver your service. For example, you may use software than comes with a hefty monthly fee.

Kellen Driscoll, a performance coach, also charges based on the value he provides and factors in the cost of inaction. "I want the value of what I offer to be 10 times or more of the investment. Meaning, if my rate were $3,000, I wanted to make sure the value I provided would help my client produce at least $30,000. This way, the cost of NOT working with me is far greater than the investment to work with me."

In some cases, you may have flexibility in your fee. Let's take a look at a few examples.

Meg McKeen is the founder and Chief Confidence Builder at Adjunct Advisors (www.adjunctadvisors.com/). In her role, she works with insurance salespeople to leverage their unique voice (and find success) in their career and life. Although she has established fees, there's a sliding scale. She explains:

> *I consider if I'm being retained by an individual or by their employer; corporations tend to have larger budgets for training and development, so I've developed scholarship programs for those paying individually in order to continue to be accessible for both.*

Irene Papajohn is a marketing expert and career coach. Like Meg, her rate varies based on the situation. "I factor in the type of client and the individual's likely financial scenario. For example, if they are out of work, I will take a lower rate because I can and I care about helping people—especially those who need the most help." While this is an incredibly kind approach, you should also consider the minimum amount you will accept for your work. Otherwise, just consider it volunteer work.

That said, you should expect some friction when it comes to pricing, so be empathetic about it. This could be a huge investment for a potential client, so it's on you to de-risk that investment for them. You do this by demonstrating a clear understanding of their problems and presenting a solution aligned with their desired outcomes. As time goes by, you'll also have referrals and testimonials to reference. However, if you notice a prospect starts talking about your price before talking about your service, that's a bit of a red flag. This lets you know they're primarily concerned with saving money and may not fully appreciate the value you have to provide.

The one exception to that red flag is organizations. Some organizations are required to ask for a discount, even if it's not crucial to signing a contract. The reasons vary; it could be part of some "best practice" finance decision to insert the request in any contract negotiation process. You have a few options in this case:

▶ Say no, but reinforce the outcomes of their investment and the amount of effort you'll need to put in.

▶ Say yes if they agree to pay faster or offer some other benefit, for example, agreeing to be featured as a case study that you can share with other prospects.

Earlier in my career, I offered extremely deep discounts to a few companies I wanted to work with. They were household names and I knew having them on my list of clients would help me get more work in the future. Of course, I couldn't do this too often or I'd be working around the clock to pay my basic living expenses. Approach each use case as it comes, but try not to get in the habit of discounting. Reason being, one of the best ways to grow your business is through referrals. If these clients refer you to other people—and mention your low rate—you'll continue attracting prospects who don't want to pay your full rate.

Setting Your Goals

The amount you charge needs to align with your revenue goals. This alignment is often overlooked, especially by new consultants.

Let's say you plan on charging $100 an hour. That sounds like a lot of money, and it can be in some cases, but let's break down how that looks over a year. This model in Figure 2–2 assumes you work for 50 weeks and take weeks of vacation.

Hourly rate	$100
Target billable hours per week	20
Target weekly income	$2,000
Target annual income	$100,000

FIGURE 2–2: **Pricing Goal Model**

This sounds great, except for the fact that it assumes you're billing a client 50 percent of the time you're working. This is certainly possible, but not guaranteed. Remember earlier when I mentioned that much of your time will be spent working on and not in your business? Well, those aren't billable hours. Also, if you're working that much, it doesn't leave a lot of time for lead generation.

This model also doesn't account for your overhead such as insurance, a coworking space, and any programs you use to run your business. Most importantly, it doesn't account for taxes!

Here's a more realistic scenario. In Figure 2–3, I break out a few more details in my model.

Hourly rate	$100
Target billable hours per week	20
Target weekly income	$2,000
Target annual income	$100,000
Taxes and overhead	($50,000)
Net annual income	$50,000

FIGURE 2–3: **Detailed Pricing Goal Model**

Suddenly, charging $100 an hour doesn't sound like that much.

I should note, another drawback of charging by the hour is that there is way too much variability in how many hours a potential client may book, or how many clients you'll need to hit your goal.

When you're first getting started, it's much easier to project revenue by selling packages or on a retainer basis. So, let's say you have a consulting package that costs $5,000. The revenue breakdown would look like Figure 2–4 below.

Package Rate	Clients per Quarter	Quarterly Revenue	Annual Revenue
$5,000	8	$40,000	$160,000

FIGURE 2–4: **Package Rate Breakdown**

After taxes and expenses, this model is much more likely to net you $100,000.

Of course, there may be some variability in how much you charge for your package. As you get more experienced, you'll be able to better understand your average deal value. In this example, a deal can be defined as a package.

Your average deal value can be calculated as total revenue divided by number of deals or packages sold. So, if you made $15,000 from three deals, your average order deal value is $5,000.

This is where your strategic planning will come into play. Once you understand your average deal value, and the percent of leads that convert, it all becomes a numbers game. You'll keep an eye on your lead pipeline to make sure you're set up for success and spend more time prospecting new leads as needed. You'll even track the source of converting leads so you can better understand the value of your marketing and outreach. We'll cover this in depth when we talk about setting up a customer relationship management (CRM) model in Chapter 4.

The amount you charge will inevitably change as time goes by. You'll hone your offering, get clearer on who you want to work with, and optimize your lead-generation activities. For now, draw a line in the sand and move forward with it. When someone asks you your rate, or how you arrive at it, don't say "it depends." Tell it to them like they asked you what time it is—be clear and specific. Your confidence is key to winning valuable deals.

Why This Is Important

During this chapter you've learned how to avoid making a common mistake, which is not having a real plan to guide your actions and decisions. Too often, new consultants dive into working on projects without a clear understanding of how it aligns with the goals and vision they have for their business and personal life.

Having a clear sense of process is the key to making the right business decisions going forward. Beyond that, clarity is the precursor to confidence, which you'll need when pitching and delivering your services.

Action Items

▶ Determine what business model you would like to use based on your area of expertise and desired lifestyle.

▶ Perform competitive and prospect research to determine how much you should charge for your services.

▶ Determine your desired gross revenue for your first year of operations.

▶ Estimate how many projects, retainer clients, or hours you would need in order to hit that goal. Make revisions as needed.

▶ Complete the Income Streams & Pricing section of The One Page Business Plan

Setting Up Your Consulting Service

S etting up your consulting service can be exciting and frustrating at the same time. You're an expert at helping people and organizations solve problems, but all of sudden you also need to figure out how to complete one form or another. Beyond that, some of the basic requirements that were previously taken care of on your behalf—such as the equipment you'll need to do your job and where you'll work—are now your responsibility.

Although some people start with determining what to call their business, deciding the name is just the beginning. You'll also need to determine your business structure, startup costs, and work environment. In this chapter, we'll walk you through some basic setup considerations that you'll need to think about when getting your consulting business off the ground.

Name Your Business

When I first started my business, I spent about an hour trying to determine the name, then realized I was just trying to look busy as opposed to doing actual work. Sure, your business name is important, but don't get too caught up on it if it's stopping you from doing something more tangible. The right idea might come to you while you're going for a walk or hanging out with friends. You can also check out *The Naming Book* by Brad Flowers (Entrepreneur Press, 2020), which takes you through a series of exercises to come up with the right name for your business.

Meg McKeen explains how she came up with the name of her business. She considered several factors when choosing the name of her company:

- ► The services she would offer and how the business name might correlate
- ► The ease of creating a memorable online presence
- ► The ability of the name to grow with her business

The work Meg does, though aligned with the insurance industry, is specific to training and development. Most insurance providers and insurance sales organizations include "insurance" in their name, so it was important to her that she fill a different need. So as not to confuse her potential clients, she specifically chose not to include the word "insurance" in the business name.

Meg says, "I also considered the services I do (outsourced training and education) and the word 'adjunct' fit perfectly as I considered the context of the word in education (think 'adjunct professor.') I then conducted a domain search and was happy to discover that www.adjunctadvisors.com was available and affordable! I chose to make 'advisor' plural to allow for future growth through affiliates or employees."

Meg makes a good point that choosing a name should allow room for expansion. If you don't, your business could get pigeonholed. For example, I suspect the founders of Just Salad would have landed on a different name if they knew how their menu would evolve over the years.

I originally went with the name "Brooklyn Digital Marketing." I live in Brooklyn and offered digital marketing services, so it was a no brainer. It also helped me rank higher in search engine optimization (SEO) for people who were looking for local digital marketing consultants. However, this name also presented a challenge because people thought I was part of a team. Sure, that sounds cool at first, but you also have some explaining to do when others ask about this nonexistent team. It also makes it more challenging to write copy for your website. "We provide . . ." versus "I provide . . ." have different connotations for prospective clients.

After a few years, I changed my business name to "Terry Rice Consulting." Again, it was not an overly creative name, but the impact was amazing. People started recognizing me as an industry expert, which led to more media opportunities. Many of these opportunities were paid.

Dr. Linda Henman, a strategy coach based in St. Louis and author of *The Magnetic Boss*, also advises choosing a name that combines your own name and the nature of your business. "Not having your name as a part of your company name deprives you of an opportunity to promote your identity," she says. "On the other hand, using your name alone misses a chance to clarify the nature of your business. I think a combination is best."

If you choose to go with a more creative approach, follow these guidelines:

- ▶ Make sure it's easy to spell.
- ▶ Determine whether or not a relevant URL is available.
- ▶ Be prepared to explain the story of why you choose that name.

Once you come up with a name, ask several people what they think about it. As a heads-up, you may need to check your ego on this one. If possible, ask people who fit the customer profile and persona you'll be targeting.

Here's a way you can start spreading the word and get help naming your company: Ask for input on social media. Just put up a brief post that says, "I'm launching my consulting business this fall, but I'm still thinking of a name, what do you think of the following options?" You can make it even more engaging by creating an Instagram story with voting options.

People support what they co-create. You may find yourself attracting your first prospects before you even launch.

Secure Your Name

Let's talk about some legal stuff. Once you've selected your business name, your next step should be to register it with your local government, usually at the county level. Most states require you to file paperwork to establish your business name as a unique "assumed name," even if you're using your own name as part of the company name. Known variously as a *fictitious business name* or *dba*, which is short for "doing business as," an assumed name establishes that you're the only one permitted to operate under that name in that jurisdiction. An assumed name is also necessary so you can accept and cash checks in your company name, as well as set up a business checking account (which is always recommended, no matter how small your operation may be).

tip

The official site of the U.S. Small Business Administration, www.SBA.gov, has a search tool on its site that will connect you to a listing of all the federal, state, and local permits, licenses, and registrations you'll need to run your business. Simply enter your city and state or ZIP code, and a comprehensive list with links will pop up.

The fee to file for a dba is nominal depending on where you live, ranging from as little as $10 to around $150. As part of the registration process, the county will do a search of local businesses to ascertain that your name is unique. In case the name you've chosen has already been taken (which most likely wouldn't happen if you include your own name in your business name), be sure to have a couple of extra names in reserve.

Apply for Appropriate Licenses

A business license is also usually inexpensive—perhaps $10 or $20—and is renewable annually. You can most likely do all this online, but this will vary based on location. It's possible you'll need other state or even federal licenses to operate, depending on the kind of work you do. For example, every state requires a Series 63 license for financial advisors to conduct business within its borders.

In your line of work, you may find the state licensing paperwork requirements to be minimal—or nonexistent. In addition to a business license, if you're a consultant in a specialized field (and you know who you are), you may need a professional license to do business. Check with the appropriate state agency for additional information and clarification.

Create Your Legal Business Structure

Now that you have a business name, you need an official business structure. I briefly offered consulting services back in 2007 without creating a real business structure. It was incredibly awkward when I tried to position myself as an expert, while also asking for checks to be made out to me personally. Having a personal Gmail account didn't help much, either. If you want to look official, be official by setting up a legitimate business structure.

Choosing a legal form of business is another one of those decisions you should make early in the business planning process. Basically, there are four types of legal structures: sole proprietorship, partnership, corporation, and limited liability company (LLC). Here's a quick rundown on each:

▶ *Sole Proprietorship.* This is the easiest and least expensive legal structure to adopt, which is why so many startup businesses begin this way. There's little paperwork—all you do is file Schedule C, Profit or Loss from Business, when you file your personal income taxes, as well as a couple of other tax forms related to business use of your home and tax payments if you choose to deduct expenses. Just keep in mind that the sole proprietor is personally responsible for all of the business debt, and both personal and business assets are fair game for creditors.

▶ *Partnership.* Under this form, two or more people share ownership of the company, either in equal or unequal amounts, and each partner is responsible for the business debt. Profits and expenses are recorded on the partners' individual income tax forms. Partnerships work especially well for people with complementary skills, but there can be disagreements about workloads, responsibility, and other matters, so it's important to have a partnership agreement drawn up before embarking on this type of venture.

▶ *Corporation.* A main benefit of a corporation is that business liability against the owner(s) is limited because it's considered to be an entity separate from the owner(s). A main disadvantage of a corporation is that you have to observe certain corporate formalities, including holding an annual meeting (although it can be at Denny's rather than in a ballroom at the Hyatt), electing officers, and issuing stock certificates. It's also more expensive to form a corporation. There are two types of corporations. The S corp is somewhat more advantageous to a small-business owner because it's taxed like a partnership and profits/losses are reported through personal income tax forms. However, you have to qualify for S corp status. You'll gain an "Inc." designation with a C corp, as well as the requirement to fill out a lot more paperwork (because of federal, state, and local requirements). Usually you'll pay higher taxes because both corporate earnings and personal earnings are taxed.

▶ *Limited Liability Company (LLC).* An LLC combines the limited liability of a corporation and the tax benefits of a sole proprietorship or partnership. It's a good choice for a small-business owner who's leery about liability but wants to avoid the corporate formalities of a C or S corp.

With all the variables involved in selecting the most appropriate form of business for your consultancy, you'll find it helpful to talk to an attorney and a CPA to assist you with the navigating the paperwork and formalities of the process.

But before you jump into paying a professional to help you get legally set up, you can do a little research into your options and all of the tasks that go with setting each one up. Check out the following resources to get started:

▶ Small Business Administration (www.sba.gov).The SBA is an excellent online resource for consultants who are just starting their own practice. Everything from advice on promoting your business to financial planning is available with the click of your mouse.

▶ LegalZoom (www.legalzoom.com). LegalZoom is a leading provider of personalized, online legal solutions and legal documents for small businesses and families.

▶ MyCorporation (www.mycorporation.com). MyCorporation is a leader in business formation, trademarks and copyrights, registered agent services, and more. Be sure to check out the Learning Center.

▶ SCORE (www.score.org). The nation's largest network of volunteer, expert business mentors is dedicated to helping small businesses get off the ground, grow, and achieve their goals.

You can also find help locally by contacting a chamber of commerce, Meetup groups, or through social media communities specific to your area.

Determine Your Work Environment

If you previously worked in-house at an organization, you probably didn't have much control over your work environment. Now that's all about to change since you are going solo, but you'll need to choose wisely. We've all heard stories about entrepreneurs who launched their business by working from a coffee shop. That may be cost-effective at first, but it may not be the best environment for you. Praying you get a seat next to the outlet isn't the best way to start your day.

Working from Home

In many cases, you'll start by working from your home or apartment. I worked from home for the first two years, and it had its ups and downs. At that time, we had an extra bedroom that I could easily repurpose as an office. I bought a new computer, standing desk, and dual monitors to make it all official. On the plus side, I wasn't spending any money on office space. I also didn't have a commute, which helped me pack more productivity into the day. However, I had trouble establishing clear boundaries on when to start and stop work. It became even more challenging once my daughter was born. At one point, I saw her little hand sliding and wiggling under the door to my office, trying to get my attention. That's when I knew it was time to get a coworking space.

If you're going to work from home, I recommend the following:

- ▶ If at all possible, select a location that has a door. In a pinch, you may want to buy a room divider or screen from a retailer that sells office furniture.
- ▶ Determine a scheduled start and end time for your business day. Remember: *You don't have to do more to be more.* Developing healthy boundaries will help you avoid burnout.
- ▶ If other people will be around the house during your work day, make sure they respect your boundaries during working hours. Consider wearing noise-canceling headphones, even if you're not listening to anything.
- ▶ If your wifi isn't overly strong, get an Ethernet adapter for your laptop. You don't want to have challenges connecting via screen share or other online platforms when you are trying to have a video call or meeting.
- ▶ Don't just jump back into conversations or activities with the people who occupy your living space; give yourself a few minutes to disconnect from work first.
- ▶ I strongly recommend an exercise routine so you don't end up sitting all day. At least get out and walk around during the day. Try to identify something new in your neighborhood every time you leave; this will also help resolve mental blocks.

However, there will always be some disadvantages to working from home. Some of those are:

- ▶ *Isolation.* If you're used to working in a large office setting with plenty of people, you may experience culture shock when you first open a home-based consulting business. Make sure you develop a network of friends and other associates you can connect with on a regular basis. Join a professional organization like the chamber of commerce, or consistently go to the same class at your gym. Anything to get you in front of familiar faces will help curb feelings of isolation and fear of missing out (FOMO).
- ▶ *The lure of home responsibilities.* You have to be well disciplined to work at home successfully. You must be able to say to yourself, "I'm at work. I will not stop working on this proposal to do the laundry, mow the lawn, or shovel the snow." Beware of minor distractions that can eat up your whole day.

▶ *Lack of meeting space.* It may be hard enough to find sufficient space for a home office, let alone a conference room. You'll probably have to make alternate arrangements when meeting with clients. It helps to have a few go-to locations handy like a meeting room at the local library or coworking space, or a coffee shop during quieter hours.

I strongly suggest keeping your office based at home as long as possible to cut down on overhead. That said, it may not be an ideal environment once your business starts growing. While it's beneficial to have a private place to work outside of the home, it's by no means a prerequisite.

Joining a Coworking Space

Once you're ready to leave, the next stop will most likely be a coworking space (which are changing rapidly in a post-COVID environment, but still an option). This is a great way to get many of the amenities associated with working at an organization. You'll have conference rooms available and various services, such as printing and high-speed internet.

Again, you'll want to choose wisely and go in with a game plan for what kind of space and services you want as well as your budget. You will find that membership plans vary from space to space. Most coworking spaces offer desks in addition to private offices. For example, many coworking spaces have "dedicated" desks and "hot" desks. As the name implies, a dedicated desk is reserved just for you. You can set your workstation up with permanent fixtures and leave your belongings at the office. A hot desk is open for anyone to use, and you can't leave anything behind at the end of the day.

Rates will vary by city, specific location, and what kind of services are offered, but here are some numbers to consider, using WeWork as an example coworking space. If you were to get a dedicated desk at the WeWork in Brooklyn Heights, the cost is around $580/mo. The cost for a hot desk is $370 per month. With a delta of $210, you're probably better off getting a dedicated desk. You'll be more comfortable and have a command center to call your own. I suspect the increased productivity would easily pay for itself.

A private office at the same location currently costs $850 per month. This is obviously a much bigger investment but also provides more space and privacy. It will be much easier to take calls and attend video conferences without a bunch of random people around you. That said, there's no harm in starting with a dedicated or hot desk. Most coworking spaces, from national brands like WeWork to local independent spaces, will offer a certain number of hours in a reserved conference room so you can schedule meetings. Many also offer mini "phone booth" style rooms where you can jump in and take calls in peace.

Like most business expenses, you're usually better off waiting to develop a need for a more premium service, so it doesn't hurt to start out with a drop-in membership to test the waters before you commit big dollars to a dedicated space.

You'll also need to determine what sort of interaction you want to have with others who use the space. Each location will have its own unique culture. Do you want to be that person who's always the first to arrive at Taco Tuesday? Or would you prefer to keep your head down and focus on work?

There are several clear benefits to socializing at a coworking space. You could make new friends, connect with prospects, and perhaps get leads for your business. Beyond that, sometimes it's just nice to reset over casual conversation. If you thrive off the energy of others, the choice is clear.

The downside is that you will need to set up boundaries. Do you want someone interrupting your day to ask if you saw the latest viral YouTube video, or reminding you that it's Taco Tuesday? These small interruptions can seriously throw off your concentration and lower productivity. According to estimates based on a recent UC Irvine study, refocusing your efforts after just one interruption can take up to 23 minutes.

To avoid these distractions, I don't consult or chat with anyone at my coworking space. I know that sounds drastic, but I firmly believe this is why I can get so much accomplished during a relatively short workday. I'll say "thanks" for holding a door or greet people—there's never an excuse to be overtly rude to anyone—but I'm sincerely not interested in discussing whether or not it might rain that afternoon. I also don't consult anyone who works in my building because I need to protect my work boundaries. I use this space to generate revenue, which supports my family. I don't want to worry about someone knocking on my door to confirm I received an email, or checking to see if I'm available for a quick chat. I know this is common when you work for a company, but you get to make your own rules now. I also meditate often. Just the thought of a potential interruption could disrupt my resetting and recovery process.

That's not to say you shouldn't socialize during the day. For me, I get my fill of it when I go to my gym, which is literally next door to my coworking space. This approach isn't for everyone; you may enjoy socializing at work. Just be sure to set up, and reinforce, healthy boundaries.

The location of your office is also extremely important. Remember: You're designing your business around your life, not the other way around. One of the main benefits my coworking space offers is proximity to my gym, my kid's daycare/school, and apartment. I can leave my office at 5:00, pick my kids up, and be home by 5:25. I also don't have an excuse to skip the gym because it's so close.

When picking a location, you'll need to determine what's most important to you:

▶ Do you want a short commute?

▶ Would you like to be near bars/restaurants so you can easily entertain or unwind?

▶ Do you like the idea of getting a quick workout over lunch?

▶ What sort of community do you want to join?

The rate you'll pay is important, but don't sacrifice your lifestyle just to save a few bucks.

Why This Is Important

Properly setting up your consulting business from the start will save you from countless unforeseen headaches down the line. Although these activities may not be related to your area of expertise, it will get you used to the back office work and additional considerations that come with being an entrepreneur. If you feel you have a strong aversion to this type of work, you may choose to outsource it down the line. For now, let's keep moving forward.

As a result of COVID, work and workplace have been decoupled for several organizations and industries. Working from home may be part of your long-term plan, so be sure to set yourself up for success by having an established work environment and daily routine.

Action Items

▶ Determine the name of your business, ask ten people directly for their opinion, and consider asking others on social media.

▶ Check to make sure the name you've decided on is available.

▶ Create a legal business entity and file all associated forms.

▶ Set up your work environment, and focus on building your business around your lifestyle.

Tools of the Trade

Work smarter, not harder. While this is good advice, it's not overly directional. Years ago, one of a consultant's most valuable tools was their Rolodex. While the strength of your network is often critical to success, there are now additional tools that can help you streamline your business process.

Although they may take some time to set up and get the hang of, implementing various applications and programs will eventually help you spend more time providing value to your target audience and less time doing administrative work.

I suggest setting up and implementing the following tools:

▶ Customer relationship management (CRM)
▶ Project management
▶ Appointment scheduling
▶ Video conferencing
▶ Email marketing

I know it may sound like we are getting to this a bit early, but you want to instill these good habits from the start. Here's a situation that happens all too often. Let's check in with our avatar, Tina.

Tina met an amazing prospect, Spencer, at her first networking event. She wasn't really planning on pitching any services, but he heard what she had to offer and was immediately interested. She wrote down all his information and made a note to call him on the 15th of the month, as planned. During the interim, Tina got caught up with numerous other tasks before realizing she forgot to send a calendar hold to connect on the 15th. She frantically got an email out to Spencer the day before but received no response. A few days later, Spencer got back to her apologizing for the delay and asked if she was free to chat. Tina agreed, even though she just got back from the gym and was not prepared for the call. She then proceeded to fumble around the conversation for the next 20 minutes. Spencer thanked her for her time, but she never heard back from him again.

Sadly, this happens far too often. You can easily tank your first (and several other) deals if you aren't prepared.

This entire fiasco could have been avoided if the right process were put in place from the beginning. Having strong, reliable processes and tools in place is critical to your success as a consultant. Many of the most successful people in the world commit to an unrelenting system or process to drive excellence. This commitment will be key to you winning deals and maintaining order. In this chapter, I'll walk through five tools that will help you streamline your business processes.

Customer Relationship Management (CRM) System

A customer relationship management (CRM) system is where you'll track interactions you have with valuable business partners, prospects, and clients. I recommend starting with the free version of a product like HubSpot.

Having all this information in one place is crucial, especially if you're a solopreneur. Here's how the scenario with Tina could have gone differently if she had used HubSpot:

▶ After she met Spencer, she added him as a contact in HubSpot. This included his name, email address, title, and website.

▶ In the Notes section of his record, she included the main talking points of their conversation.

▶ She then created a Task to do research on his company and industry prior to their call on the 15th. She set up a reminder to make sure this was completed before the 13th.

▶ Tina also sent Spencer an email, which included a calendar hold for the 15th.

▶ Adding this to her pipeline, she created a Deal for this opportunity, which references the estimated value of the deal.

▶ Just before her call with Spencer, Tina referenced the notes she took during their initial chat as well as the information she discovered while researching his company and industry.

▶ After the call, she tracked this as an activity (which will be associated with his record) and planned next steps.

This is the process you need to follow with every relevant opportunity, no matter what kind of CRM you use. Nothing slips through the cracks, and you have all the information needed at your disposal.

For all Deals, it's crucial you enter the Lead Source, which shows how you connected with the prospect in the first place (social media, networking, referral, etc.). As you begin to close deals, you'll be able to attribute the source of this revenue and tailor your prospecting activities accordingly. For example, you may notice 80 percent of your closed deals come from free events you spoke at. This information will easily justify the value associated with getting in front of your target audience, even if you're not being paid to do so at the time. The more specific information about the lead source, the better.

tip

When you select the Sales view in HubSpot, you'll be able to see all your upcoming Tasks and the value of Deals added to your pipeline.

Access to this data also allows you to forecast revenue for upcoming time periods and make adjustments to your service offering as needed.

For example, one of my clients was originally providing a social media consulting package for $250. If she wanted to make $100,000 per year before taxes, she would have to sell 100 of these packages per quarter! Even if her close rate (the percent of deals won) was 50 percent, she'd still need to pitch 200 prospects per quarter. It doesn't matter how robust your CRM is built out, that approach is unrealistic. Instead, we put together a package that cost $5,000. Now she only needs five clients per quarter, and she can spend more time with her son.

Setting up and leveraging your CRM system may seem challenging at first. Like any new routine, it will take some getting used to. However, this is all part of running a real business. With your CRM in place, you'll be able to accurately predict revenue trends and identify additional areas of opportunity. Check out the onboarding resources provided by HubSpot at https://www.hubspot.com/services/onboarding.

Project Management

You're going to be busy, which involves working on numerous projects. These can be individual projects or collaborations with other businesses and, of course, your clients. With so much going on, you need a dedicated system to organize, track, and manage your work. This is where project management systems come in handy. Through one tool, you'll be able to see all the workflows, people, and assigned responsibilities associated with all your projects.

For example:

- ▶ Collecting any information needed before starting the project
- ▶ Detailing the steps needed to complete various project milestones
- ▶ Storing documents and other files for easy access
- ▶ Tagging specific individuals in comments and making them aware of action items

Although there are several available, I use Asana (https://asana.com/). There's a free version that provides several valuable features. According to their website, this application allows you to "Easily organize and plan workflows, projects, and more, so you can keep your team's work on schedule."

Here's an example of how I use it with my own consultancy. One of the best ways to get in front of your target audience is by speaking at conferences or other industry events. However, you need to develop at least one go-to, signature speech before pitching. A *signature speech* is an educational and persuasive presentation that will impact your audience's personal and/or professional life. You'll spend a great deal of time creating and refining it, which is why you want to make sure you pick the right topic. One way to pick your topic is to research organizations who book people like you and get an idea of what those speakers are talking about. From there, you'll need to determine how you can best add value to the conversation. The next step involves creating an outline and eventually writing the entire speech.

This process involves a lot of moving parts, so I use Asana to track all these activities and deliverables.

The organizational hierarchy is as follows:

Section

  • Task

    – Subtask

      ○ Notes and documents

Here's how it would look for the signature speech":

Signature Speech

  • List of relevant events

    – Speaking topics

      ○ Notes about topics, contact information for event organizer

As a coach, I can make sure my clients are following through with the project we agreed on and offer input along the way. They can also directly assign action items to me; I'd then get an alert making me aware of this.

I've also used Asana to collaborate with other service providers. The woman who built my website used it to outline all the sections, then asked for my input on specific copy for each page. She even added due dates to make sure we hit our expected launch.

Additional use cases include:

► Planning a corporate event
► Implementing a new CMS
► Designing a new inventory management workflow
► Tracking action items and progress toward getting a better night's rest

To see the tool in action, head to my website (www.terryrice.co/bookresources)

Appointment Scheduling

Time kills deals. If you volley back and forth trying to figure out when you can connect with a prospect, you can easily miss out on a great opportunity. So, it's important to make sure that you schedule appointments efficiently and proactively.

Here's an example of what *not* to say when booking time with a prospect: "It was great meeting you; I'm looking forward to exploring how we can work together."

This is a vague way to set up an appointment. It leaves the prospective client in the dark about what to expect from your next interaction. Instead, specifically address when you are looking forward to exploring more with them. You need to provide your specific availability.

Here's a slightly better approach: "It was great meeting you; I'm looking forward to exploring how we can work together. I'm available Tuesday from 9:00 A.M. to 12:00 P.M. EST and again from 2:00 P.M. to 4:00 P.M. EST. If that doesn't work, I'm also free Wednesday from 1:30 P.M. and 5:00 P.M. EST."

This is a slightly better approach, but what if your availability changes? Or, what if none of those times work for the prospect?

Again, all this kind of back-and-forth causes friction in the communication process. One of your greatest strengths as a consultant is ease of doing business, so don't make it difficult just to schedule a meeting. Here are some appointment-setting programs and apps you can use to make life easier for you and your clients:

▶ Calendly
▶ Boomerang
▶ ScheduleOnce
▶ Acuity

I use Acuity (https://acuityscheduling.com/) for scheduling appointments; it is a Squarespace company so it integrates well with my website. I simply indicate my availability throughout the week, then share it with anyone who may need to book time with me. Since it syncs with my Google calendar, my availability is always up-to-date. No double booking!

Acuity also allows you to set up different appointment types. This is how you indicate the purpose of your meeting or the service you'll be providing. I currently have the following appointment types:

▶ *20-Minute Discovery Call.* A free call used for connecting with potential clients. I have everyone complete an intake form so I can do some research in advance. This includes basic information such as their website URL, LinkedIn profile, target audience, and the services they provide.
▶ *30-Minute Meeting.* These are great for booking a standard meeting with existing contacts.
▶ *60-Minute Meeting.* I use this for extended meetings with existing contacts, coaching calls, and media opportunities.

One of my favorite features is the ability to provide different availability based on the purpose of the call. I always prioritize my existing clients when it comes to availability. You can even provide a direct scheduling link for specific appointment types; this prevents people from signing up for a meeting that isn't aligned with the intended use case.

You can also use Acuity to schedule paid coaching calls, which clients can pay for through the application, or free "discovery" calls for prospective clients.

You may be opposed to providing a free discovery call. You may be concerned about giving away too much information for free. While this is a healthy concern, you have more to offer than what could be delivered in 20 minutes. Beyond that, the goal of this call is to get an understanding of your prospects challenges, then consider ways you may be able to assist. If you're doing more talking than they are, you'll need to adjust your approach. We'll cover this in depth in Chapter 12. However, if you notice a prospect keeps asking for specific strategies, as opposed to asking more about you and how you help people, that's a very serious red flag.

Along those lines, you may be concerned that you'll waste your time on people who aren't a good fit. There are a few ways to combat this. First, be very intentional about who you're attracting. Do you only work with nonprofits? Say that on your website, repeatedly. Second, use the intake form as a filter. You could have a field that says, "I focus on helping certified nonprofit organizations. Does this apply to you?". If they say "no," politely cancel the appointment.

Your intake form should also ask how they were made aware of you. Mine currently states:

How did you hear about me? (If applicable, please indicate a specific social channel, website, or event.)

It's important to keep track of all your discovery calls within HubSpot (or your preferred CRM) so you can track the outcomes. Again, you may be exposing the sign-up link to the wrong people. Referencing your link while speaking at a free event that attracted 500 people may net you a lot of booked calls but may not convert as well as speaking at a paid event that only had 50 attendees.

Over time, you'll start to see patterns and align your actions with desired outcomes.

Setting up an appointment-scheduling system may take you an hour or two, but it will save you a lot of time and help you win more business going forward. You'll also have more time to focus on the core activities that you enjoy and are central to the success of your business. Taking time out of your day to schedule meetings is a distraction from operating in your zone of genius that can be easily avoided with the right process in place.

Video Conferencing

Sure, meeting in person is the best way to forge genuine relationships, but it's not always possible for a variety of reasons. Video conferencing is the next best thing. You can still pick up on and deliver many nonverbal cues via a video call. The ability to share screens often comes in handy as well so you and your clients can view the same documents at the same time. Some video conferencing programs you can use are:

▶ Google Meet
▶ Skype
▶ GoToMeeting
▶ Zoom

I use Zoom (https://zoom.us/) for video conferencing. Like many of the tools I've discussed, there's a free version available. You can easily integrate Zoom with Acuity, allowing you to seamlessly set up video calls. If you'd like—and the other person agrees—you can record the conversation. I typically only do this during coaching calls since it puts less pressure on my clients to take notes. They can focus on being present instead of documenting.

Since you'll be on camera, you obviously want to make sure you're presentable. I usually head to the gym while I'm at my office, so I keep an extra shirt around just in case I need to be on camera that day. You'll also want to be aware of your background. The reflection from windows or people walking behind you can be a bit of a distraction. If you have challenges with lighting, I also suggest buying a selfie light. You can get one for under $30 and you'll look a lot better on camera. Along those lines, you want to make sure there are no issues with your audio. You may be able to get by with the headphones that came with your phone, but investing in something more advanced could prove beneficial. I wear Bose noise-canceling headphones and Blue Microphone's Yeti USB Microphone. Together, these can easily cost over $400, so I'd only invest in these once you develop a need to do so. I appear on podcasts frequently and like having a more professional setup, which is why I eventually went this route. For now, just make sure people can see and hear you.

One last note about video conferencing: Remember, your prospects are picking up on your verbal cues, even when you're about to sign off. You'd be surprised how many people go from looking friendly to not so friendly at the end of video conference, and it's all caught on camera. It's understandable, you may be returning to a packed inbox or need to prep for another call, but it's a horrible last impression to leave. I always close warmly, and keep smiling *until the session has ended.*

Email Service Provider

While some entrepreneurs are obsessed with amassing a large number of social media followers, this effort can easily be in vain. Followers aren't leads. You can contact leads when you choose to and easily track those interactions. Followers may or may not see your content, and it's juxtaposed against many other pieces of content when they do.

This is why you need to develop and nurture your email list. We'll get into the specifics of that in Chapter 10. For now, we'll address how you're going to deploy these emails through an email service provider (ESP). Fortunately, like many other CRM systems, HubSpot can also serve as your ESP. If you have that implemented, you'll most likely want to use this as opposed to another platform. You'll have fewer logins and integrations to worry about, which can be a time saver.

There are several email programs available including:

▶ ConvertKit
▶ Constant Contact
▶ Drip
▶ Campaign Monitor

That said, MailChimp is a popular choice among small businesses and entrepreneurs. The platform is very intuitive, and there are numerous resources available to help guide you along the way. Beyond that, MailChimp has a very large and active user base, so you can often find the answers to specific questions in a community forum.

Either way, you need a real ESP. Don't just send mass emails from your Gmail account. You also need to make sure you're following regulations around how you can communicate with recipients. If not, you could find yourself in hot water. In the U.S., commercial emails are regulated by the CAN-SPAM Act. This law sets the rules for commercial email, establishes requirements for commercial messages, gives recipients the right to have you stop emailing them, and spells out tough penalties for violations. Each separate email in violation of the CAN-SPAM Act is subject to penalties of up to $42,530. One of the most common violations is not allowing people to unsubscribe from your list. When using an ESP, this option will be made available in every email. This obviously isn't the case if you mail directly from a

tip

It's important to note that some products may overlap in regard to their features. Use as few tools as possible, but you can typically "connect" one tool to another if needed. If a direct integration isn't available, you can often use Zapier (https://zapier.com/) to automate the process.

platform, such as Gmail. MailChimp has great resources on their website to keep you out of hot water, and they provide a direct link to the FTC regulations at https://mailchimp.com/help/anti-spam-requirements-for-email/.

Beyond that, ESPs provide you with powerful data, letting you know who's opening and clicking your emails. This allows you to optimize your outreach and reduce the number of people who unsubscribe.

Why This Is Important

Choosing all of these tools can seem intimidating, and it's not necessarily what you signed up for when you decided to launch your consulting business. Your goal is to help people, not to become an expert at various tools and apps. It's important to remember that these tools of the trade will give you more time to work with your audience and will help you do so more efficiently. If needed, you can bring in another consultant to help you implement these tools and teach you how to use them properly.

Action Items

- ▶ Implement your CRM, project management, appointment-scheduling platforms, and video conferencing platform.
- ▶ Plan on implementing your email marketing platform one week before you "officially" launch.
- ▶ Read guides and watch tutorials so you can learn how to properly use these tools.
- ▶ Consider getting help with implementation, if needed.

Establishing Your Credibility

For an established professional, it can be frustrating to have to prove yourself in your new role. However, it's extremely important, so don't let that frustration become a roadblock to progress. If you're not yet an established name in your field, be extremely clear with prospective clients about what you're capable of so you meet their expectations. That whole "fake it till you make it" approach is exhausting and could easily damage your reputation before you even get started, so stay clear of overhyping your skillset.

Remember: You judge yourself based on what you believe you're capable of. Other people judge you based on what you've already demonstrated. Beyond that, you should always be growing as a professional. Engaging in conversations with other professionals is one of the best ways to do so. Keep in mind, these people don't have to be in the same industry as you. In fact, borrowing best practices from another industry may be what sets you apart from the competition. This chapter is all about establishing your credibility so you can be recognized and rewarded for your expertise.

Although I had a fair amount of experience in my industry when I began consulting, the way I initially presented myself wasn't doing me any favors. I thought dropping names about where I used to work and the clients I worked with would be enough to start acquiring clients. Sure, it helped, but I still needed to establish my foundation as an independent consultant. There's a big difference between being good at your job at an organization and being able to successfully operate a consulting business. Beyond that, you need to establish your own brand. You can't keep associating your expertise with the company you used to work at. That involves constantly going backward, and your new role will require much more innovation and forward thinking.

Meg McKeen, the insurance salesperson consultant, provides an excellent example of this: "I already held a revered insurance-related designation and many years in the industry, so my credibility was already deep. Training (coaching specifically) was a new focus for me, so much of my time spent on professional development was (and continues to be) spent in honing my knowledge there." It's important to keep in mind that although you may be an expert at what you do, you may not be an expert at teaching others how to do the same.

Irene Papajohn, the marketing expert and career coach, shares a similar experience. "For marketing, I have my MBA and over 15 years of experience. For coaching, I studied positive psychology coaching and took workshops around emotional intelligence and leadership. I studied these areas for myself—it isn't something that I tout anywhere." Sure, it's great to have industry-recognized certifications—it helps with branding and attracting the right audience. But, as Irene shares, the true benefit is being able to better service your clients.

Let's go back to the example of Tina. After failing to win her first client, Tina was understandably a bit disappointed. She wondered if she had what it takes to be successful, or if she needed to get another college degree to be seen as a professional. In her case, getting another degree probably isn't necessary. In fact, it's probably a waste of time and money. However, there are steps any consultant can take to increase their credibility.

In this chapter, we'll walk through how to increase your credibility through certifications and community or professional memberships. We'll also discuss professional development opportunities, which will be one of your most valuable investments.

Credentials and Certifications

After reviewing the websites of other people in your industry, you may have noticed many of them reference various credentials and certifications. If so, you may want to consider doing the same. Based on your area of expertise, there may be legal or regulatory requirements around achieving some credentials. For example, you obviously can't call yourself a psychologist without a proper degree.

Early in my career, I worked as a search engine marketing (SEM) consultant, which involved helping clients monetize paid search ads. The gold standard for this area of expertise is being Google Ads Certified, which involves passing a series of online tests. It was—and still is—incredibly challenging to get a job in paid search without this certification. It was all potential clients had to go on when trying to gauge whether or not someone was qualified for the role. These days, HR representatives still look for this certification when scanning resumes and LinkedIn profiles. Needless to say, if you were pursuing a career as an independent search engine marketing consultant, it's a must-have.

Industry-recognized credentials set you apart from the crowd and can help you win business. They prove you've invested time—and potentially money—into proving and developing your expertise. It signals to colleagues and prospects that this is your profession; you're not just a novice trying to get by.

Here's where it gets challenging. Pretty much any institution can offer a "certification" as long as they're not falsely indicating they're an accredited college or something along those lines. Watch out for certifications that nobody has ever heard of, or ones that throw off any sort of red flags. Trust your gut on this one. Your certification isn't overly valuable if you have to continually vouch for its credibility.

Another option is to simply ask other people in the industry. Is there a Facebook group or Reddit community you can post in? Many of your competitors will gladly provide you with valuable information about what kinds of certifications are valuable in your industry. There's enough business to go around for everyone.

I should note that although certifications can be valuable, that doesn't mean people are going to hire you just because you have them. You still have to put in the work to prove your expertise. I've encountered many people who are certified on one platform or another but can't apply that knowledge to meaningful work. Let your certifications be a reflection of your bona fides—not the only valuable element of your professional identity.

Local Business Organizations

You've probably heard several times that entrepreneurship can be lonely. Joining a community of other professionals is a great way to build meaningful relationships and pick up some valuable tips. It can be tempting to immediately go into prospecting mode. Don't. You'll project a scarcity mindset that will easily turn people off, especially if they're just meeting you for the first time. This is a good piece of advice to carry into any situation, but it's especially important as you're initially building your reputation.

Instead of selling, focus on learning. When networking with local groups, pay attention to:

tip

Instead of asking people what they do for work, ask them what they do for fun. Then, ask follow-up questions. Don't just wait for an opportunity to talk about yourself.

- ▶ How other people are presenting themselves
- ▶ How they package their services
- ▶ How they market their business
- ▶ What tools they are using

Let people know what you do, but make it clear you're there for the experience. This relaxed approach is extremely refreshing to other attendees. So much so, you may find some people start asking probing questions about your services, which could lead to a future opportunity.

I became a member of the Brooklyn Chamber of Commerce about a month after launching my business. They sent me a welcome kit, which included a plaque I hung up in my home office. Nobody outside of my family was ever going to see it, but it reinforced the feeling that I was running a legitimate business. Having the logo on my site helped increase my credibility as well.

Functionally, being a Chamber member gave me an immediate reference group. I would head to networking events, start to see familiar faces, and gain insight into how other professionals ran their businesses. No matter what professional group you participate in, consistent attendance is key. Over time, you'll start to see the same people over and over, which deepens the relationship.

This membership can give you access to the member directory, which you should take full advantage of. Using the directory, you can email hundreds of other local businesses, which can lead to securing clients. More importantly, it led to me forming business relationships that I still maintain to this day.

A quick Google search will show you other small-business-oriented organizations in your area. In New York City, for example, we have the NYC Small Business Services. This organization helps New Yorkers start and grow businesses. They offer multiple free classes throughout the month, which I also turned into networking events. Look for similar opportunities in your area. At this stage, professional development is one of the most important investments you can make. You may also meet allies who can assist and encourage you as your business grows.

Make sure to bring business cards to organization meetings. You can get some made for around $10 using services like Vistaprint (www.vistaprint.com), and Moo (www.Moo.com) offers higher-end options at a more premium price point. Just make sure you have something that describes what you do, who you do it for, and an easy way to contact you. Some people aren't fans of business cards, and that's fine—just make sure you have some available for the people who are. When you receive a business card from someone, be sure to jot down a note about them so you can reference this during your next conversation.

tip

Don't get business cards that are glossy on both sides. It's difficult to write on a glossy surface. If you give your card to someone, they won't be able to jot down additional information. Stick with a matte finish.

One of the most important things you can do is to seek opportunities to volunteer for these organizations or join leadership committees. You'll meet more members and increase your visibility. Does your local organization have a new member welcome committee? Join it! You'll have an excuse to form a relationship with everyone who becomes a member after you.

Industry-Specific Organizations

If there is a well-known organization for your industry, you should strongly consider joining. This will give you a great opportunity to learn from and network with other professionals, while also boosting your credibility.

For example, if you're a digital marketing consultant, the American Marketing Association (https://www.ama.org/) could be a great fit. With more than 70 professional chapters across North America, you can network with other professionals and exchange ideas about what's happening in marketing. A professional membership costs $300 and comes with discounts on various products and services.

Joining an industry-specific organization will often provide you with more actionable takeaways when compared to a local business organization. However, you may be among people who offer the exact same services, so there's a bit more competition when it is time to start selling.

Once you get your feet wet with general membership, you can try to join a committee or other high-visibility position. Even if it's unpaid, you'll still boost your credibility and gain exposure to more members as a thought leader within your organization.

tip

Another option is to lead a survey of members and publish your findings. You'll have an excuse to contact several members and gain recognition for summarizing their input.

Online Groups

Although you often make deeper connections in person, joining relevant online groups is the most accessible option for most people. This may be your primary connection point if you don't have a robust business development community in your area or have other constraints that make attending in-person events a challenge. I don't attend nearly as many in-person networking events as some of my peers because they often take place at night, and I'd rather be home with my family. Fortunately, I was able to acquire the majority of my initial clients through online interactions. Of course, during the COVID shutdown, this was the only way many of us could network. I suggest joining a mixture of industry-specific groups, as well as general business-development-focused groups. The more people you connect with, the more allies you'll have out in the field when it comes time to make more connections and prospect new clients.

On Facebook or LinkedIn, you simply have to search for terms that include [your industry + consultants]. For example, you could search for "sustainability consultants." Many of these are free, even if the admins are eventually trying to sell you something. Be respectful of people's time. Try not to ask questions you can search for on Google, or at least ask for other's opinions of what you've discovered.

You'll also want to follow relevant hashtags and profiles, including those found on Twitter and Instagram. Although these may not be traditional memberships, it will still help you develop and maintain a connection with the professional community.

Carefully consider any social media groups, especially if they require you to pay for membership. Ask:

▶ Who is leading the conversation?
▶ How often do they post?
▶ Who else is in the group? Are they your peers?
▶ Is this my preferred style of interaction?

When managed properly, paid or private groups tend to provide more value than free or open groups. The group admin is on the line to curate a robust community, which results in higher quality content and engagement. For example, I initially paid about $600 to join a private Facebook group that focused on best practices for Facebook ads. Along with group membership, I was also able to attend weekly coaching calls with the admin and watch previous calls on-demand. The value I gained far exceeded my investment. I was able to interact with and learn from a group of my peers. Through these interactions, I was made aware of all the latest updates I may have missed for one reason or another.

Conferences and Industry Events

Investing in yourself is crucial, but paying big money to attend pricey conferences or industry events is one you may need to hold off on, depending on your financial situation. Some of these events cost thousands of dollars to attend in addition to travel expenses, so you need to be prepared to get your money's worth. The main advantages of attending in-person events are the information you gain and the connections you'll make. I would argue the latter is even more important. The event is more or less an opportunity and filter for you to meet people who can help you develop personally or professionally. Again, don't project lack and scarcity by trying to sell yourself too soon. People pick up on this easily, and it's a major turnoff. Instead, use this as an opportunity to build a network that you'll nurture over time.

Use this as an opportunity to start a relationship with the event organizers, too. Connect with them in person or send them an email providing feedback about the event. These connections will come in handy if you want to be on stage at their next event.

To further amplify the impact of attending conferences, jot down some of your takeaways from each section and write a blog about it. Then, tease out some of these insights on social media, and tag the presenter in the post. They may see this and share with their followers as well. Just like that, you're on your way to growing your visibility and credibility. Get in the habit of doing this at every event you attend and you'll build a solid network over time.

Why This Is Important

As an independent consultant, you're building a personal brand. Being aligned with well-known organizations is one way to do so, but the genuine connections you make with others will be extremely beneficial as well. You'll learn by watching how people introduce themselves and describe their business.

You'll also discover you're not the only one who faces challenges and doubts themselves at times. Entrepreneurship can be lonely, so you'll need to have a network of people you can reach out to when necessary. And, of course, this network could be an amazing source of leads as you build your consulting practice.

Action Items

▶ Research competitors, and determine any certifications that you may want to obtain.

▶ Determine local business organizations to join, and find opportunities to volunteer.

▶ Consider joining industry-specific organizations, and find opportunities to volunteer.

▶ Join relevant online groups, and actively engage with other members.

▶ Consider attending conferences and industry events, and focus on building relationships.

Positioning
and Packages

The Entrepreneur.com Small Business Encyclopedia
defines *positioning* as "How you differentiate your
product or service from that of your competitors'
and then determine which market niche to fill." Positioning
helps establish your product's or service's identity within
the eyes of the purchaser. Here's a great example. Meg

McKeen (who you first met in Chapter 2), founder of Adjunct Advisors, LLC, trains insurance salespeople.

Meg can attest to the benefits of providing clarity to your audience: "By being so specific about who I serve and the value I provide, my ideal clients know quickly if I am for them or not. As a result, more often than not, prospects are approaching me to engage."

Without proper positioning, it's hard for people to determine whether or not you're the right fit to solve their problems. Your positioning should attract your ideal audience, while letting others know you wouldn't be able to help them.

Packaging refers to how you'll deliver your service. In Meg's case, she offers a few options:

- ▶ One-on-one training
- ▶ Group training with other individuals
- ▶ Facilitated workshops for an established group or team

Celia Arias is a startup COO and operations strategist (www.celiarias.com). She offers the following packages:

- ▶ Business Operations Audit & Recommendations
- ▶ Business Operations Audit & Recommendations + Implementation
- ▶ Business Operations Audit & Recommendations + Implementation + Ongoing Support

If a prospect asks Celia how she can help, she'll say, "I demystify business processes, so you can scale easily and get back to enjoying your passions."

The response Meg and Celia provide is known as a positioning statement. You'll develop yours shortly.

In this chapter, we'll cover how to develop your positioning statement, service offering, and a predetermined cost for these services. We'll also walk through best practices for communicating with prospects and following up with proposals. Get ready—this part is challenging and exciting at the same time. Let's start by talking about what a positioning statement is and why you need one.

Your Positioning Statement

What do you do, and for whom do you do it? As a consultant, you should be able to answer this question in about 25 words or less. This is often referred to as a *positioning statement.*

Your positioning statement must include:

▶ What you do
▶ Who you serve
▶ The transformation the client seeks

While my wife and I were trying to determine what pre-K program we wanted our daughter to attend, we came across a consultant who assisted with this specific problem. At the top of her website it said:

I help parents find affordable schools that meet the educational, cultural, and recreational needs of their children.

That's all I needed to hear. $300 later, we felt much better about a new and daunting process. This consultant's positioning statement was clear, direct, and persuasive. That's what yours should be, too.

Here's my positioning statement:

I help entrepreneurs and consultants monetize their knowledge so they can grow their business without sacrificing their health, family, or personal interests.

This statement needs to not only lure the right people in for more information but it should also turn away people who aren't a good fit for working with me. In my case, I'm not able to help entrepreneurs build an app or secure financing, and my positioning statement doesn't mislead people into thinking I do. But, if they want to get paid for consulting, speaking, or associated revenue streams, I can assist.

Here are a few other examples of positioning statements:

This one comes from Jake Savage, a Fundraising Strategist (https://jakesavage.co/):

I teach fundraising teams how to be more persuasive and win bigger donations.

Jake realized the majority of clients he worked with didn't have a challenge connecting with donors; they just needed help being more persuasive. He specializes in helping them be more persuasive without being pushy. The end result is to close bigger donations, and he specifically mentions this in his positioning statement.

Here's another example from Amina AlTai, the holistic business and mindset coach:

I teach female leaders how to come home to themselves and anchor in their purpose so they can do work they freaking love, feel good, and get paid.

Notice that she explicitly addresses women leaders. All the content on her website specifically mentions women as well. Amina hints at her personality, and the people she wants to attract by saying "work they freaking love." Sure, this may turn off some prospects, but she's not interested in connecting with them. Your positioning statement should be polarizing by design so you attract the client base that best fits your personality and offerings.

Anna Vatuone, a personal brand strategist (www.annavatuone.com) keeps hers short and specific:

I teach entrepreneurs how to build their personal brand using social media.

In practice, Anna and her agency do much more than that. Among other things, she can develop your website, create a logo, and also assist with setting up your CRM system. But she knows building brands on social media is her main area of focus, and it can easily lead to these other opportunities.

If she said, "I teach entrepreneurs how to build their personal brand using social media and assist with setting up your website and your CRM system and . . ." it would be extremely confusing. Besides that, every "and" you include in your statement in regard to audiences or services can reduce the impact by half. When hiring a consultant, prospects want to work with people who are knowledgeable and continually learning about their area of expertise. It's challenging to maintain a high level of expertise when you focus on so many skills or industries.

Your positioning statement also needs to include implied or specific outcomes. What will clients get by working with you? What outcomes can you add to your positioning statement? Examples may include:

> tip ⓘ
>
> Admittedly, focusing on one niche is debatable and contextual. Some clients may prefer to work with one resource as opposed to many, and you may have more than one skill set to offer. Feel free to experiment and make adjustments as needed.

- ▶ Increased revenue
- ▶ Reduced spend
- ▶ Improved health
- ▶ Social status
- ▶ Time saved
- ▶ Clarity
- ▶ Less stress

Whatever outcomes you choose to include, the more clearly it is aligned with your target audience's needs or aspirations, the better.

Your positioning statement must meet the following criteria:

- ▶ Easy for you to remember. You shouldn't fumble around when saying it.
- ▶ Easy for your network or prospects to remember. People can't spread the word or make a decision if they can't remember what you do.

▶ Quickly allows people to understand whether or not you're a good fit for them. It should act as a filter to save your time and a potential prospect's time.

Let's go back to the example of our avatar, Tina. Here's what she came up with as a positioning statement:

I help small businesses increase their revenue and retention by implementing customer relationship management systems.

As you can see, this hits on all the criteria we've discussed thus far. It's important to remember that your positioning statement is not an elevator pitch. You're not pitching anyone; you're just giving them information in a concise manner. If they want more, they'll ask for it or continue browsing your site. You can then expand on it a bit.

For example, here's what I have on my website:

I help entrepreneurs monetize their knowledge so they can get paid for who they are, not just what they do. This includes landing consulting opportunities, paid speaking gigs, and other knowledge-based services. I have a five-step process that addresses your critical needs, and I'll be there to guide you along the way.

This is getting very close to a traditional elevator pitch, but it still focuses on your audience, not you. To create this additional content, think of a concise way you would respond to someone who heard your positioning statement, then asked for more information.

Process and Packaging

When coming up with his process and packaging, Kellen Driscoll leveraged what he had observed in his industry, without spending too much time polishing his approach.

I looked at my own experiences as well as the coaching and consulting programs that I had personally invested in. I also had to be realistic of where I was at in my business. I did not need to have it all figured out. I just need a client, then another client, then another client.

Like Kellen, the way you present yourself will evolve over time. You just need something to get started.

You may have a great positioning statement, but are unclear about what you would do if a client asked about your process for achieving the outcomes referenced. This happens quite often. Back when I did digital marketing audits, I could easily find ways for companies to optimize their campaigns, but it was more of an art than a science. One time, a client asked if he could watch while I went through the process and was confused about why I appeared to just be poking around. Sure, I knew I had to look at their targeting, bidding, and creative, but I didn't have a checklist in front of me to guide my actions. If I tried to explain my process before he hired me, I probably wouldn't have won the business.

One of the most important elements of being a good consultant is having a defined process. What journey are you going to take your clients on that eventually leads them to their desired outcome? You need to lay these tracks in advance, making sure you address all of their concerns along the way. For example, if you were teaching someone how to boil eggs you'd say:

▶ Get a pot.
▶ Put eggs in it.
▶ Fill it with water.
▶ Turn the stove on.
▶ Place the pot on the stove.
▶ Wait six minutes.

This is a very simple example, but you get the picture. Remember, it's important to explain this from their point of view and use language they would understand. So, you wouldn't say "cauldron" instead of "pot."

What you don't need is some super mystical proprietary formula. Clients don't want unique approaches; they want to be understood. Once you understand them, they want to know you have a plan that will solve their problems or meet their aspirations. That's it.

Your processes needs to be explained in a way that is simple to understand, even if it will take a sufficient amount of effort to implement. Clients want to know that you have an established framework for success and you're not just making things up as you go along.

The process chart in Figure 6–1 shows how I define the process for my consulting program.

| Clarity and Vision | We'll nail down the services you offer, how much to charge, who you offer them to, and why you're their obvious choice. |
| | You'll be able to confidently interact with your target audience and turn down opportunities that aren't aligned with the vision you have for your life. |

FIGURE 6–1: **Process Chart**

Process	Focus on doing what you love by implementing routines, apps, and services to streamline your business process.
	This includes implementation of customer relationship management platform, allowing you to better track deals and forecast revenue.
Branding and Marketing	Learn how to position yourself, provide value to your audience, and perform "passive prospecting" through social media, in-person events, and podcast appearances.
	You'll discover how to get in front of your audience in a way that doesn't feel salesy or desperate.
Pitching and Proposals	I'll supply you with training and templates to make this part simple, pain-free, and predictable.
	You'll also learn how to put your clients' needs first and describe the return on investment or return on effort they can expect.
Fulfillment	From onboarding to relationship management, I'll teach you how to deliver on the promises you've made with a systematic approach.
	This includes setting up online folders and templates and providing tools for your clients.

FIGURE 6–1: **Process Chart,** continued

You'll notice this book is designed the same way very much. Here's an example of how it looked when I consulted companies on Facebook marketing (see Figure 6–2).

Campaign Objective	Determine the correct objective to select, based on your company and campaign goals.
	Go beyond basic interests to reach a more qualified audience.
Audience Targeting	We'll cover custom audiences, retargeting, and lookalike audiences.

FIGURE 6–2: **Facebook Marketing Process Chart**

Budgeting and Bidding	Discover how to budget based on your audience and overall goals.
	You'll also learn how to control your cost per action by bidding your true value.
Ad Creative	In a noisy social world, thumb-stopping content is vital to success.
	We'll walk through how to create content that gets people to stop scrolling and start engaging.
Campaign Optimization	During this phase, we'll scale your budgets while still maintaining your KPI targets.
	Through A/B testing, we'll be able to continually explore and refine campaigns.

FIGURE 6–2: **Facebook Marketing Process Chart,** continued

Here's how it could look for Tina. See Figure 6–3.

Scoping Conversation	Focusing on your overall business goals, we'll begin by reviewing your current business processes and flag any areas that may impact sustainability or scalability.
Transformation Plan	I'll document and identify the critical business challenges that need to be solved for and create a new road map aligned with identified goals.
	We'll then implement tools and processes to execute on the road map.
Solutions Implementation	Implement tools and processes discussed in the Transformation Plan.
	Onsite training for staff to ensure product adoption.
	Ongoing email support and weekly check-ins to monitor implementation and identify any additional needs.

FIGURE 6–3: **Tina's Process Chart**

Implementation Audit and Review	I'll review the outcomes of the CRM implementation and make any needed adjustments.
	I'll also address any additional training questions that arise.
Ongoing Support	Optional retainer-based support, addressing any ad hoc questions or support needed.

FIGURE 6–3: **Tina's Process Chart,** continued

While each use case is different, most processes follow a similar approach of determining goals and challenges, outlining a solution, implementing it, and providing ongoing support.

You don't have to follow this exact approach, but you need something set up in advance before you start talking to prospects. You can easily lose a potential deal by coming off as unprepared. I've found some consultants have a great amount of raw talent and they're naturally good at solving problems, but they struggle to grow due to the lack of a defined process. Avoid this mistake by developing and committing to a process. Fortunately, you've picked up some valuable tips from all the research you previously conducted.

In most cases, you'll want to develop various packages, each offering different levels of service. If you only have one offer, the only thing a prospect has to say "no" to is everything. Sure, they might ask for some adjustments, or they might just keep it moving.

With my consulting program, I originally offered weekly coaching calls. Some people said they wanted to be in the program, but weekly calls would be too time consuming. Conversely, some prospects told me they wanted to meet more often. I eventually made packages that satisfied both needs, while also maintaining the option for a bespoke solution. These bespoke solutions take more time to create, but it's better than saying "take it or leave it."

Let's say you deliver advice that helps your client solve a problem, but you could also help with implementation. In the case of the school consultant, she could help you determine what school to go to and offer to help you fill out the applications for an additional charge.

It's beneficial to have an offer that's way more expensive than the other options because somebody might actually buy it and it makes the other options look cheaper.

Just make sure you're willing to do whatever is outlined!

Figure 6-4 on page 74 shows an example of how that could look.

Package	Price
Business Operations Audit & Recommendations	$5,000
Business Operations Audit & Recommendations + Implementation	$14,000
Recommendations + Implementation + Ongoing Support	$14,000 + $2,000/mo

FIGURE 6–4: **Offer Outline**

The amount you charge will be based on the service you provide and the time it takes to deliver these services. In this case, the audit and recommendations might take a relatively short period of time, but the implementation process could be long and complex. When possible, you should always try to include ongoing support as an option. This is essentially a retainer model and can be a great way to generate consistent income after the initial project has been completed.

Why This Is Important

You may tweak some or all of this several times. That's perfectly normal. The most important thing is to have something documented. You'll feel much better navigating any conversation and start to feel more like an established professional. Beyond that, you'll attract more potential clients by sounding sure of who you are and what you have to offer.

Your positioning statement is a hook line that draws clients in, giving you the opportunity explain how you help them based on their own unique situation. Make sure it's about them and not about you. Your process and the way you package your service help you create an irresistible offer designed to meet the needs of your specific audience.

Action Items

- ► Research positioning statements from other independent consultants or individuals who serve your target audience.
- ► Draft your positioning statement, share it directly with 10 people, and get feedback.
- ► Define your process, and describe how you'll sequentially take clients from where they are to where they want to be.

▶ Research service packages offered by other independent consultants or individuals who serve your target audience.

▶ Develop your service package, get feedback, and revise as needed.

▶ Complete the What services do you offer, What is your solution at a high level and Positioning Statement sections of The One Page Business Plan.

Launching Your Website and Social Channels

Your online presence is often the key to connecting with prospects you haven't met before, turning those prospects into leads and reinforcing why those leads would eventually want to work with you. When set up correctly, you'll be able to automate this entire process without paying to advertise or spamming people's inboxes.

Again, you're building a personal brand, so your website and social channels are a representation of that brand. We won't be talking about posting on LinkedIn five times a day or mastering some complex algorithm to get more views of your content in this book. But we will discuss how you can integrate maintaining your online presence in a way that doesn't feel forced or salesy.

However, it's not imperative to have a website or even a large online presence. If you look at Kellen Driscoll's LinkedIn profile, it says he's a performance coach and his most recent work experience was playing in an Arena Football league from 2007 to 2010. However, he's been able to sustain a lucrative consulting business for over five years.

You will likely decide to have a website, but that doesn't mean you have to build it yourself. Howie See is the president and founder of Strategic F1 where he provides strategic direction to any size of business. He offers his advice as you're just getting started:

> *If you have the means, pay or get help from a professional to do certain aspects of your business instead of wasting massive amounts of time trying to do it by yourself. Your time can be spent doing what you do best. Taking 20 hours to try to figure out how to set up a website that looks like a child created it (instead of paying someone a few hundred dollars to set up a simple site) is not the best use of your time."*

Irene Papajohn reinforces why a website shouldn't be a barrier to launch. "I know people who start with their website and cards, etc., but I got my first client before any of that." So while we're covering all these aesthetics, don't feel like you need to do them in sequential order.

Now that you have finalized your positioning statement, process, and packaging, it's time to start putting yourself out there more. Having an online presence isn't an option; it's a requirement. In this chapter, we'll cover a detailed process that allows you to get this done with little to no technical or marketing background.

Create Your Website

My first website looked horrible. Seriously. It looked like someone ate a bunch of other websites and vomited them all over the screen. I paid a guy I found on Craigslist $250 to do the design and still didn't get my money's worth. Nobody's website is perfect, but you can avoid some common mistakes by aligning with a vetted professional or using templates from companies like Wix or Squarespace. Your website could easily be the first and last impression someone has of you, so make sure it's a good one.

You may be tempted to skip the task of building a website until you get more traction for your business. Guess what? *This is part of building that traction.* You need an online home you can point people toward when they want more information about you and the services you offer. That said, don't let perfection be the enemy of progress. I've seen many people delay the launch of their business because they make endless tweaks to their website. You have plenty of time to make adjustments. For now, you have to be okay with something that's presentable so you can get started marketing your consulting business. You're about to start meeting peers and potential clients, so you'll need this set up in advance.

Before you get started, I suggest reviewing at least 10 websites of other people in your industry. Consider the following:

▶ What are some common themes you'd like to adopt?
▶ How much content do they have?
▶ Do they provide tools or resources?
▶ Do they include videos or a sizzle reel?

In regard to content, you'll want to keep it brief initially. Otherwise, you run the risk of taking forever to launch. The main sections you'll need are:

▶ Homepage
▶ About Page
▶ Services
▶ Contact
▶ Blog

Let's explore each one.

The Homepage

This is the first step toward branding yourself, because it is the first thing people will see when they visit your site. Think of the homepage like the front door to your online "home." If possible, you'll want to have a high-quality photo of yourself at the top of the page. I suggest using your positioning statement (which you read about in Chapter 6) as the headline. Right away, people will know who you are and how you can help them.

Mine says this:

Get Paid for Who You Are, Instead of Just What You Do

I help entrepreneurs and consultants monetize their knowledge so they can grow their business without sacrificing their health, family, or personal interests.

Clearly, that requires some explaining, but it does a solid job of framing my service. I then provide additional context further down the page.

Accelerate your growth—get access to the critical resources and guidance you need to succeed.

Do you need help finding clients who value you as a business partner, not just a service provider?

Would you like to monetize your knowledge through conferences, workshops, and podcasts, but aren't sure how to make it happen?

Do you need someone to help you streamline your business development process, so you can focus on providing value for your audience?

I've helped hundreds of entrepreneurs monetize their knowledge so they can get paid for who they are, instead of just what they do.

The content should directly reflect what you learned while creating your empathy map (which you read about in Chapter 1). Express your understanding of your audience's journey and how you can assist them, and provide some sort of credentials or reinforcement of your expertise. Figure 7–1 shows an easy formula for you to use.

You know how . . .	Your audience's current situation, the reason they need an expert's help
Well, what I do is . . .	Your service offering
In fact . . .	Proof of your expertise, why they should choose you.

FIGURE 7–1: **Homepage Formula**

Figure 7–2 shows how this could look for Tina.

You know how . . .	It's incredibly challenging to run your business when you're not sure where your leads are coming from, or how much revenue you'll be bringing in next month.

FIGURE 7–2: **Example Homepage Formula**

Well, what I do is . . .	Help small businesses reduce uncertainty and increase their revenue by implementing customer relationship management systems.
In fact . . .	I've been doing this for over five years as an in-house operations expert.

FIGURE 7–2: **Example Homepage Formula,** continued

If you can nail down this part, you're well on your way. If you can't, you'll need to revisit the research you've already done on your audience.

It's beneficial to detail a few scenarios in which you can be of assistance using phrases like:

▶ "Maybe you have this challenge . . ."
▶ "Or perhaps this is what keeps you up at night . . ."
▶ "I've also been able to help people in this situation . . ."

Your goal is to establish yourself as the go-to resource for the challenge the prospect is experiencing.

Then, go into detail about how you can specifically help them. Don't assume they'll click on a "Services" link. However, be sure to focus more on them and their problem as opposed to talking about you and your solution.

If you have testimonials, this is a great place to show them off. However, this may not be possible in the early days of your business. Instead, consider adding quotes from people you've worked with in the past. In the short term, this content will still provide valuable social proof.

Here's an example:

I had the pleasure of working with Nick for years at XYZ corporation. His natural inclination to ask questions before jumping into solutions helped us deliver stunning results for our clients.

You'll also want to make it extremely easy for people to contact you. Consider embedding a contact form on the homepage, or making a clearly visible link on the main navigation menu. Don't just put your email address and expect them to write to you—that causes friction in the communication process. A visitor would have to draft an email just to get in contact with you, and they may not include all the information you need. I know writing an email isn't overly labor intensive, but some people will find it inconvenient and decide not to reach out.

Lastly, it's incredibly important to have a clearly visible lead magnet. A lead magnet is content that provides so much value, your target audience will exchange their email address to acquire it. This can appear on your homepage as well as most other pages on your website. However, you most likely don't want it on your contact page since the visitor already has the intent to contact you. Here are some examples:

▶ Toolkits/resource guides
▶ Free mini-course
▶ Checklists
▶ Templates
▶ Infographics
▶ Worksheets
▶ Webinars
▶ Video content

A good lead magnet:

▶ Provides real value to a specific audience
▶ Demonstrates your expertise
▶ Includes a call to action

Currently, my lead magnet is a free guide mini-course titled "Attract and Convert: How to Get More Consulting Clients." Once a visitor signs up, they'll gain access to a six-day course that guides them through the process of getting leads from their defined audience. During the course, they get one video from me per day that includes a video and instructions for an assignment they need to complete. At the end of the sequence there's a call to action letting them know how they can continue engaging with me. This process is more aligned with overall marketing, which we'll talk about in Chapter 10, but you should strongly consider this approach if it's a good fit for your audience. You'll always have something of high value to share with your audience and will grow your email list as a result. Beyond that, you'll be able to build a relationship with them during the course, which may make them feel much more comfortable moving forward after you present them with an opportunity to continue engaging.

That said, you don't need to hop right into creating a course. It will come out much better once you've had time to interact with your audience more. Previously, my lead magnet was a guide titled, "The 10 Biggest Mistakes Entrepreneurs Make on Social Media and What You Should Do Instead." At the end of the guide, I encouraged readers to learn more about my consulting services and potentially book an enrollment call.

Take a look at the websites of other entrepreneurs who offer professional services; this will help you get a better idea what lead magnet you would like to offer as well. You may need to partner with a graphic designer to make sure it's presentable and on brand. Or you could potentially create your own by using a service like Canva (www.canva.com). Either way, the investment will be well worth it. This lead magnet is the key to putting your prospecting on autopilot by allowing you to turn website visitors into leads. You'll also be able to reference it on social media, encouraging followers and viewers to head to your website. Lastly, a lead magnet is critical whenever you're doing cold outreach. It allows you to provide value in exchange for a prospect's attention.

Don't rush the process of developing your lead magnet. Do some research to determine what would provide the most value to your audience. Again, your empathy map will come in handy here. You can also ask around the network you've already started to form.

Keep in mind, your lead magnet will most likely change over time. You may want to experiment with a different approach, or the audience you want to work with may change. Regardless, it's important to track the source of these leads in your CRM system. You'll then be able to determine the conversion rate from one approach versus another.

Lastly, your social channels should be readily visible in the footer. I suggest having these on every page of your website. To make for a cleaner look, you can simply use the platform icon instead of the full name.

Your About Page

As you can imagine, your About page is vital to making a connection with your audience. Just being qualified isn't enough—that's a prerequisite. Your audience needs a clear understanding of your "Why" and to learn about your personality as well.

Originally, mine was more or less a rehashing of my resume. "Terry Rice has been in the industry since blah blah blah." I then connected with a branding expert, Nick McArthur of Epic Danger (www.epicdangerblog.com). He showed me how to differentiate myself from other consultants by simply reflecting more of my personality.

Here's an example of the additional content I added:

In my free time, I enjoy listening to Audible and going to CrossFit. As you probably know, the first rule of CrossFit is finding an excuse to talk about it.

Some of my best (self-assessed) qualities are curiosity, grit, and a constant focus on impact. I'm also extremely solutions oriented. My approach to most challenges can best be summarized as "It is what it is. Now, what's the best thing we can do from here?

I can't stress this part enough. Prospects are using this content to determine whether or not they want to start a relationship with you. Give them the information they need! This is also the best way to attract people who value you for who you are, not just what you do.

You'll also need a decent headshot or photo on your page. I highly recommend getting this done professionally. Depending on where you live, you can probably get something decent for less than a few hundred dollars. If you need something in a pinch, a quality photo taken with your phone will do for now. Just be sure to think about how you're presenting yourself. Look professional (no photos of you at Disneyland), and be sure to smile in your picture or at least look somewhat happy; you'll look much more approachable. I originally had a headshot that was taken for free at a conference where I looked capable but wasn't smiling. Once I switched it out to a friendlier photo, the conversion rate on my contact page doubled.

tip

This is also a great place to reference your social handles. You can even show some of your most recent social posts, as long as they're appropriate and relevant.

Services Page

Here's where you'll explain what you have to offer to prospective clients. But don't just start talking about yourself; you'll still want to put your audience's needs and concerns first. It's beneficial to start with a question that speaks to their needs when you are laying out your menu of services.

The headline for my services page is as follows:

Discover how to attract clients and opportunities that will pay you what you're worth.

Learn the five-step process for developing, packaging, and promoting services built for your defined audience.

If you'd like to optimize your headline for search engines, it's beneficial to include what your audience is searching for in the title or headline. If you can do so without it sounding weird or obvious, go for it. Another option is to routinely mention questions your audience may Google in your blog section. For example, I wrote a blog called "How to Find a Coach for Consultants: Your Five-Step Process for Aligning with the Right Mentor."

tip

Adding another photo of yourself is beneficial here as well. It will help humanize the content and reinforce who they'll be working with.

The keywords I'm trying to optimize for are "coach for consultants" (more on this later when we talk about your blog on page 86).

Of course, you'll need to reference the services you offer. Be careful not to fall into the traditional marketing trap of talking about features and benefits. Talk about the current situation your audience is experiencing, the plan you've developed to help them, and the outcomes they can expect. Clearly outline the transformation you can help them achieve. In this case, it's beneficial to hypothesize.

I state the following on my website:

Imagine what your life could be like if:

▶ *You never have to cold-call or chase after a lead to get them on the phone.*

▶ *You know exactly what your services are worth and aren't afraid to ask for it.*

▶ *You work only with clients who respect you.*

▶ *You're not constantly stressing about generating revenue.*

What transformation is your audience looking for? It's beneficial to list between three and five possible outcomes. They may not all be applicable to each prospect, but you'll increase your chances of creating a moment of relevance if prospects can see themselves in the outcomes you present.

Next, it's time to describe the services you developed in the previous chapter. Again, you should clearly state what you do as it relates to their challenges or desires. The flow should be: Their situation → Your process → Their outcomes.

Include plenty of calls to action (CTA) on your Services page, but keep it focused. Don't ask people to join your email list, attend a free webinar, and schedule an enrollment call. All of those options can be confusing and prevent them from doing anything. Instead, think about what specific action you want the prospect to take, and craft your CTA language to encourage them to move forward. In my case, I want prospects to schedule an enrollment call. Why? Because I know those are the

tip

If you have testimonials, this is a perfect place to put them. Including photos of the people you've helped is great but not necessarily a requirement at this time. Just make it clear these are real people, and be prepared to provide their contact information, if requested.

people that are most likely to book my services in the near future. Sure, some people who join my email list eventually become clients as well. But it takes longer and the conversion rate isn't as high as a traditional CTA on the Services page. Enrollment calls convert faster and at a higher rate, so I offer this opportunity five times on my services page. Focus on the one thing you want them to do, and make it easy for them to do so.

Contact Page

You've already provided multiple opportunities for people to contact you all over your site. However, some visitors will instinctively look for a contact page. Provide a form for them to fill out. If you want to provide your email address or other information, do so as an image, not text. There are various programs that can automatically scan your site and add your email to a distribution list if you show it as text, which will greatly increase the amount of spam mail you'll receive.

Start by reminding visitors of what you're offering. Mine simply says:

I am available for consulting, workshops, and speaking engagements.

Just want to say hi? Fill out the form below, and I'll be sure to follow up.

I then have the following fields:

▶ First Name
▶ Last Name
▶ Email Address
▶ Checkbox (Consulting, Workshop, Speaking Engagement, Other)
▶ Message

All fields but the last one are mandatory.

I suggest not adding much if any additional information. At this point, the visitor is about to contact you. No need to cloud the conversation, which could be distracting.

Blog

If you don't enjoy writing, creating a blog can be a challenge. The work you put in here will pay off big time, even if you don't consider yourself a writer. From an SEO perspective, adding a blog will help you passively attract visitors to your website. Your blog will also reinforce your expertise, making it much easier to convert readers into clients. This is one of things you'll need to push through to get done; it will separate you from everyone who tries to get by with just the bare minimum. Fortunately, the content you create can be repurposed on social media, so your efforts will scale beyond your website.

A great blog starts with having a content strategy, which is the planning, development, and management of content. This discipline can get very deep, very quickly, but we'll focus on keeping it simple and effective for now. To plan your blog, you need to tackle two major tasks. First, you need to think of ten questions your audience has and then create content that answers those questions.

Let's go back to the example of Soda, the Sleep Health Educator. She could answer questions such as:

▶ What is the best pillow to help you sleep?
▶ Will drinking alcohol help me go to sleep?
▶ What is the cure for insomnia?
▶ Does warm milk help you sleep?
▶ Is melatonin safe?

This two-step process is easy to understand, but takes great effort to execute. Again, this is where you'll separate yourself from everyone else who tries to phone it in. I'll say this in another way: If you follow this advice, you will be able to attract and win opportunities much easier than if you don't. If you're feeling a tug saying, "I still don't want to do it," consider that a trigger, reminding you this is your opportunity to truly lean into entrepreneurship and set yourself up for sustainability.

Here's how you can come up with those ten questions:

▶ Refer back to your empathy map.
▶ Google "tips for + whatever problem you solve or service you provide."
▶ Take a look at some of the blog content from consultants who offer similar services.

This last option may seem counterintuitive. If someone already answered the question, why should you do it? Will it seem like you're copying their approach? Gary Vaynerchuk spoke to this in his book *Crushing It* (Harper Business, 2018) when he said, "every story has already been told, but it hasn't been told by you." This statement is obviously true and liberating at the same time. There's absolutely nothing wrong with writing about a question that's been answered multiple times. It's your own experiences and way of communicating that make it unique. One of the most popular blog posts on my website is "Five Questions Every Consultant Must Ask During a Sales Call." I'm sure there are thousands of variations of the same blog out there. Part of what makes mine unique is that I stress the need to only work with clients with whom you truly want to partner. Even when you're selling your services, you're still the buyer. Did you catch the fact that I called it a "sales call" instead of an "enrollment conversation"? That's because I'm thinking about SEO when I'm writing my blog titles. "Sales call" gets more searches than "enrollment call." If you'd like to test out your keywords, you do so by using Ubersuggest (neilpatel.com/ubersuggest). Ubersuggest is a free SEO tool that specializes in generating new keyword ideas.

In addition to creating content, you should also consider curating content. This involves finding relevant content and packaging it for your audience in a way that allows you to provide your unique perspective. This is a great approach for people who dread writing. In the example above, I could have Googled "questions to ask during a sales call," then selected the five existing articles already online I felt would provide the most value. In this situation, I would avoid sharing responses from anyone who offers the same service as I do. It's important to credit who created the original content and not try to steer people toward an alternative to what you have to offer. Following this approach on a consistent basis will help you rapidly develop content while also forcing you to routinely read content that's relevant to your audience.

Aim to get ten pieces of content on your website before officially launching, but don't let that be the enemy of progress. Once you launch, aim for one new piece of content per week. While this may sound ambitious, it will make your social media strategy much easier (which you'll read about in the next section).

Additional Thoughts on Your Website

Your website doesn't have to be perfect—it just has to be presentable, especially when viewed on a mobile phone. Ask ten people to take a look at it and provide feedback. Here are great questions to start with: "What do you think I do? Who do you think I help?"

If they can't answer that, you have some work to do. Be sure to ask people who have an understanding of your target audience and/or industry. Critical input is more valuable than well-intended praise. If you don't change a few things after this feedback, that's a bad sign. Either you're asking the wrong people, or you can't take a hint. I can tell you from experience, you'll definitely have to check your ego when soliciting this feedback.

Launching Social Channels

Once you have your website, you'll naturally want to think about engaging with your audience on social media to drive more traffic to your site and business. Social media can be both a gift and a curse for consultants.

It's a great way to build your brand and make connections with your audience by providing value. It can also be confusing and a huge waste of time if you're not doing it right. This is why my lead magnet is an ebook, *The 10 Biggest Mistakes Entrepreneurs make on Social Media and What You Should Do Instead.* Earlier, we talked about curating content instead of solely creating it. For my ebook, I personally interviewed some of the top minds in entrepreneurship and social media and included their input. This is the perfect time to share some of their input. We'll start with Neil Patel, bestselling author and cofounder at Neil Patel Digital.

Entrepreneurs should avoid trying to build a large social following so their company can become more well known or they can become famous. Being famous doesn't guarantee an increase in revenue.

What you'll quickly realize is that the majority of your followers won't convert into leads or sales. For that reason you should focus on gaining quality followers . . . ones who are interested in you and your company.

I can't stress this point enough. Too many consultants worry about gaining followers and likes as opposed to clicks and leads. You're better off having a relatively small following that truly values what you have to say and can potentially leverage your services.

This next tip comes from Jason Feifer, editor-in-chief of *Entrepreneur*:

Remember your audience. People often think that social media is about them—their thoughts, their experiences, their whatever. But it's not, if you're doing it right. Social media is about your audience. Your social feed is functionally a small publisher, and publishers identify an audience and then relentlessly serve them. Think about why people follow you. What are they looking for? What do you represent to them? Then deliver that over and over and over again.

It's not about you. If you approach each post with the intent to provide some sort of value to your target audience, you're well on your way to finding success. You'll need to do this consistently to provide a reason for them to continuously engage with, and share, your content. I should note, the term "value" is vague by design. Yes, you should certainly provide content that answers their questions, but you'll also want to reflect who you are as a person. For example, I often say you shouldn't neglect your health, which is why you'll see videos of me working out on Instagram.

Anna Vatuone, personal brand strategist, chimes in on this one:

There are three things that people need from you in order to buy from you. They need to like you, they need to know you, and they need to trust you. There are thousands of professionals who are competing for the same clients and customers; they offer the same service, at a similar price, and they know just as much as you, too. Do you know the one thing you have on them? It's your personality. When you show your audience your authentic self, it will give your business a major competitive edge and hyper-attract the clients you want to work with.

People won't partner with you if they can't trust you. The best way to earn that trust is by being an authentic version of yourself online, not trying to portray what you think people want to see. That's where smart social media strategies come into play.

Many entrepreneurs, consultants included, focus on "seeming" as opposed to "being." In other words, they focus on the image they portray—not on actual lived experience. Instead of just seeming like this incredibly successful or knowledgeable person, which can be exhausting, focus on providing value in exchange for your audience's attention. The easiest way to attract and engage quality followers is to think of ten questions they have, then create content that answers those questions. Does this sound familiar? That's because you already did it earlier in this chapter when you read about creating a blog post. You can now repurpose your blog content as a social media post. Here's an example of how you could do that with the "Five Questions" article by creating a post about it on LinkedIn.

Are you a consultant? In my latest article, I share the five questions you must ask during every sales call. You'll learn how to better understand a prospect's needs, without sounding salesy or desperate. One of my favorite questions: What would need to happen in order for you to feel good about our results?

I'm curious: What questions do you typically ask?
(link in first comment)

OK, so now let's break down how this works:

▶ Start with a question, which identifies your target audience.
▶ You can also identify a need they have. "Need help figuring out what to say on a sales call?"
▶ Tell them what your article is about.
▶ If you don't identify your audience with the question, the title of the article can do this for you.
▶ Provide a teaser about what they can expect.
▶ This part is important! Provide value first, then ask them to click to your website. You have to prove this is worthy of their attention.
▶ Ask for their input.
▶ Social media is meant to be social. Simply asking a question will make this more of a conversation as opposed to a monologue. Also, the more comments you get, the more people will see your content.

- ▶ Add the link to your article in the comment.
- ▶ LinkedIn will restrict the reach of your post if you include a URL in it. Reason being, they don't want people clicking off the platform.

If you already answered ten questions in the form of blog content, you have over two months' worth of fresh content for social media. Just post once a week and be sure to keep an eye on all the comments you receive.

Now that we've covered use cases, we'll discuss more of the nuts and bolts associated with setting up your social channels.

Setting Up Your Accounts

Start by determining your username. Ideally, this will be some variation of your name or the name of your business, and it should be consistent across all channels. You don't want to be *Mark Johnson* on twitter and *markjohnson_3* on Instagram. Using the same name makes it easier for people to find you and you'll be able to say, "Find me on social at markjohnson" without specifying a channel.

In my case, *terryrice* wasn't available, so I went with *itsterryrice*. Fortunately, my name is relatively short so it works. If yours is longer, you can consider truncating. So, markjohonson could be mjohnson, if available.

 tip

You should also use the same high-quality photo across all channels. It will make it easier for people to recognize you and reinforce your brand.

Posting Content

How often should you post social media content? That question comes up quite often. While there is no magic number, consistency is the key to getting any results you can optimize from. I'll provide guidance to get you started shortly, but we'll start by talking about how you should engage with the content others produce.

I'm going to get extremely tactical here since this same approach can be applied to several channels. We're going to walk through the "$1.80 Strategy" developed by Gary Vaynerchuk. Here's how it works:

- ▶ Start by searching ten relevant hashtags.
- ▶ For example, you could follow #consultants and #entrepreneurship.
- ▶ Locate the top nine posts for each hashtag.
- ▶ Leave a meaningful comment (your two cents [$0.02]).

Here's a quick formula that explains why it's called the $1.80 Strategy:

10 hashtags * 9 posts * $.02 = 1.80

The overall goal is to get you to engage with your ideal audience in a targeted and meaningful way. As a result, you'll increase your network on LinkedIn and followers on other channels. The key is to leave a meaningful comment. Don't just "like" posts or say something basic like "great post!"

For example, if you see someone mention a new tool that can help them save time, you could say something to the effect of:

Thanks for sharing. I'm always looking for tools that help me save time so I can focus on doing more valuable activities. How long did it take you to get the hang of it?

This is a genuine comment and should solicit a response from the original poster and/ or other viewers. What you don't want to do is "status jack," which is the process of taking over someone else's post to serve your own agenda. Here's how this could look:

Thanks for sharing. As a business development consultant I strive to help my clients increase their efficiency and revenue through a scalable process. I have a link in my bio for an ebook you should all check out. I'll tell you the . . .

You get the point. People see right through this, and it's not the way to make a name for yourself. If you can add value to the conversation while pointing to something relevant you've developed, that's great, but make sure you're doing so in a sincere way.

Now let's dive into the specific use cases of each channel.

Using Direct Messaging

Of course, one major benefit of social media is the ability to connect with and direct message prospects without having their email address. Don't abuse this power! Jake Savage has developed a three-step process for connecting with prospects on LinkedIn. However, they can also be applied to other channels.

Don't Talk About Yourself

Number one, don't talk about yourself. People get tons of spammy messages sent to them every day and it's all the same. Here's an example.

Hey Carl! I noticed you're in the food and beverage industry. Over the past 12 months, our service has helped more than 50 businesses just like yours double their revenue!

Do you have a few minutes to chat this week? I'd love to show you how it works!

This is sad. What's even more sad is that they'll likely send a different version of the same message two days later, filling up your inbox with more noise. The reality is that people won't care about you or your service until they know that you truly care about them.

It may be tough not to mention anything about your product or service, but if you execute these steps properly, then the person will reciprocate by asking about you. That will be your time to shine.

Give a Genuine Compliment

This will require some research on your part. Find something about them that's compliment-worthy and let them know in a genuine manner. Also, make it specific. Avoid general statements like, "I wanted to compliment you on building a successful business!" That looks and feels like total BS, because it is, and they'll know it immediately. Discover something about them that you find truly intriguing. Then let them know why you find it intriguing. What you're essentially doing here is establishing rapport. This is important because that rapport will ultimately evolve into the trust that will serve as the foundation for your future partnership.

Ask a Genuine Question

If you seem genuinely curious about the person or what they do, they'll gladly respond to your question. Why?

Because most people are not jerks. We enjoy helping others because it in turn makes us feel good about ourselves. Therefore, if you ask a genuine question out of genuine curiosity, people will actually be motivated to respond!

This response will open the door to further communication. Once you have a dialogue going, they'll be more receptive to hear about your product or service.

Here's an example of how that could look.

Hey Kim, I know I'm totally coming out of the blue here, but I have a quick question for you. I noticed you've been posting a lot of value-driven content on LinkedIn lately. Your post about how to avoid burnout was particularly useful to me. I'm wondering, have you ever considered sharing your experience and point of view on podcasts?

In this case, I gave a genuine compliment and asked a genuine question.

These tips may seem simple but they do require some patience and diligence. You'll have to spend time on each potential client that you message. The time will be well worth it, though, as you start to see genuine responses roll in. These responses will lead to rapport, trust, conversation, and, eventually, a partnership.

Another approach I've seen work is to lead with value, such as that lead magnet you've developed. In this case, you won't ask for their email, but you'll provide a link for them to access it. Here's how this would look.

Hi Kim,

I took a look at your profile and noticed you run a retail business here in Brooklyn. I put together a handy guide that you may find helpful: "5 Ways Non-Experts Can Leverage Social Media to Increase Foot Traffic." I'm happy to send it your way or just connect in general.

This approach provides value but is transactional at the same time, which is obviously a departure from the process Jake described. This process may turn some people off but will also quickly let you know whether or not it's working.

The point here is, there's more than one approach. So long as you're tracking the results, you'll discover what works best for you and your audience.

Now let's dig into the nuances of each social media platform.

LinkedIn

This is the go-to platform for B2B. According to Neil Patel, 80 percent of B2B leads come from LinkedIn, with another 13 percent coming from Twitter. In many cases, you could exclusively use this platform and still be successful. But don't approach it assuming everyone is just waiting to hear your pitch. This is a place to start real relationships with prospects as well as fellow entrepreneurs. Play the long game—don't be shortsighted.

Along with posting your own content, following the $1.80 Strategy is an ideal approach. I often look for "Recent" posts in addition to "Top" posts. If a relevant post was published a few minutes ago, that's a great time to engage. The author may still be online—and happy to get a response—so you may be able to start a dialogue in the comments. This could easily continue as a direct message, leading to a more formal conversation.

Following relevant hashtags also allows you to share content your audience may find valuable. When doing so, be sure to offer commentary. Don't just share it and say, "Great article!" Shared content that offers some editorial comment gets far more reach and engagement. Again, you'll want to prequalify why someone should care to read the article, and you'll get a chance to highlight your point of view.

Here's another way to strategically grow your network: Join relevant LinkedIn Groups. These could be local associations, industry-specific groups, or even niches that align with your personal interests. I found one called "Cycling Professionals" that comprised of professionals from several disciplines. So, if you're a cyclist, this could be a great fit. Sure, the majority of people in the group may not be able to help you grow your business, but you'll have a more genuine way to connect with those that can. Plus, you'll learn to see LinkedIn for what it is: a social channel that allows you to connect with professionals based on your desired criteria. Just like any other channel, it doesn't have to be all work.

Of course, sending connection requests is a more direct way of growing your network. When sending a connection request to people you don't know, provide a note in addition to the request. You have a few options:

▶ Give a compliment or ask a question.
▶ Provide value and ask to connect.
▶ Explain why you're reaching out.

Something along the lines of "Hey, I noticed you run a retail business in Brooklyn, and I'd love to learn a little more about each other," technically counts, but it's also vague and templated. As Jake said, the more effort you put in here, the better.

Here are some more quick tips for getting the most out of LinkedIn:

▶ Be sure to add a cover photo in addition to your profile photo. Show yourself speaking to a crowd or something that reflects the service you provide.
▶ Use keywords in your title and bio that your audience might search for.
▶ Here's my initial suggested posting frequency. Please note, this is just to get you started with something. Post two times per week.
▶ Comment five times per week.

Twitter

This is the spot to be for trending news and voicing your point of view. When it comes to posting, keep your content short and punchy. There's a 280-character limit, and people are used to more to content that delivers quick immediate value.

If you need to provide more context on a topic, you can tease out some of the takeaways in a post and then link back to your website or another resource.

In regard to interaction and outreach, you can follow many of the same approaches outlined for LinkedIn. However, in some cases people tend to be more responsive on Twitter as opposed to LinkedIn, especially if you @mention them in a post. They'll likely be more compelled to respond since other people can see they've been mentioned, which increases the tendency to follow social norms by replying. Beyond that, you'll most likely be on LinkedIn more than the average person. If you previously worked in-house, I imagine you weren't on the platform every day.

Again, follow relevant hashtags and make your profile discoverable by including relevant keywords.

One feature you'll definitely want to leverage is Advanced Search. With this tool, you can search for content that includes the following:

- ▶ All of these words
- ▶ This exact phrase
- ▶ Any of these words
- ▶ None of these words
- ▶ These hashtags

You can search on an account basis including:

- ▶ From these accounts
- ▶ To these accounts
- ▶ Mentioning these accounts

You can also filter by the amount of engagement and define a time period for your search.

If desired, you can search for consultants asking for social media tips and have an excuse to share your ebook, whitepaper, or other lead-gen material. Or you can look for consultants asking for input on sales calls, then share your article or blog post. You can even save these searches so they're easier to execute going forward. This will be extremely valuable if you decide to launch a speaking career. You can simply save the query "call for speakers" and monitor the results on a regular basis.

Here are some more quick tips for getting the most out of Twitter:

- ▶ Run Twitter Polls (with the built-in Twitter Polls tool). You can then share the results in a blog post.
- ▶ Retweet content from individuals and organizations you would like to partner with.
- ▶ Post one time per week.
- ▶ Comment five times per week.

Instagram

People want to work with individuals they know, like, and trust. Instagram is the perfect platform to display your personality. No need to make it all business.

One of the most unique benefits of this platform is Instagram Stories. These Stories allow users to share photos and videos to their Story, which is visible to their followers and potentially others who are following the hashtags included. One of the main benefits of Stories is that they disappear after 24 hours. As a result, there's less pressure to make the "perfect" content and you can experiment more. This ease of production allows you to consistently crank out content.

Asking questions is one of the most powerful tools you have available. You can ask your audience what questions they have about a specific topic or what content they would like you to write about next.

Amina AlTai, a holistic business coach, regularly uses the "Questions" sticker to hold office hours. This sticker allows viewers to enter free-form text, which Amina can then read and reply to. To go the extra mile and further reflect her personality, she records a personalized video response to these questions. For consistency purposes, she does this every Tuesday.

The Poll sticker is another great way to ask questions. This is a tool for getting yes or no answers to specific questions. For example, you can ask, "Would you be interested in a free webinar about . . ." If you get enough yes responses, you know you've come up with a topic people will enjoy.

You can also use the Quiz sticker to test their knowledge and show why they may need your help. Here's an example:

How many hashtags can you use in an Instagram post?

A. 5
B. 15
C. 25
D. 30

Currently, the answer is D. If a viewer responds with the wrong audience, you've already prequalified their need for your service!

To make this more strategic, you can answer many of the common questions you've heard or discovered via research.

Soda, the sleep health educator, could ask what percent of people can properly function off of four to five hours of sleep. If you're wondering, the answer is 3 percent.

Amina AlTai could ask her audience how long it takes to feel the impact of meditation. Again, if you're wondering, it takes a few weeks.

Another benefit of Stories is that you are more likely to get meaningful responses from your audience by way of direct message. Followers are sometimes less likely to provide this information as a comment on a newsfeed post, especially if it's a sensitive topic.

By design, Feed Posts are also a bit more on-brand and planned out than a Story. They're also more likely to net you new followers. I should note, the $1.80 Strategy was originally created for Instagram, so you'll definitely want to leverage it here.

Here are some more quick tips for getting the most out of Instagram:

▶ Include a call to action in your bio, such as a link to your lead magnet.
▶ Reshare relevant posts from other creators as a Story. They might share your share, increasing your overall viewability.
▶ Post a story three times per week.
▶ Comment five times per week.
▶ Post in the feed two times per week.

Facebook

Previously the go-to platform for pretty much everything social, it can be challenging to gain traction on Facebook when you are reaching out to potential consulting clients. Business pages on Facebook used to reach as much as 40 percent of your followers. These days, it's closer to 4 percent as Facebook is now prioritizing content from your personal connections and the groups you belong to. Of course, you can also post from your personal page, but that could easily annoy your "friends" who don't fit your target audience. If people don't engage with your content, Facebook won't show it as often, so it will still be challenging to get a sufficient number of eyeballs on your content.

Given these constraints, posting valuable content in relevant groups is a great strategy to adopt. We found the school consultant I previously mentioned in a Brooklyn parents Facebook group. Although it was clear what she did, she wasn't overly salesy. She would just post useful updates from time to time. For example, she posted about the deadline for applying to kindergarten. If you follow this same approach, people will view you as knowledgeable as opposed to salesy.

You can even consider creating your own group, but realize you'll need to recruit members and manage it as well. This management involves starting and monitoring conversations. As a bonus, you can do regularly scheduled Facebook Live videos, similar to the Office Hours approach used by Amina.

Here are some more quick tips for getting the most out of Facebook:

▶ Use Facebook Live for your office hours.
▶ Include a call to action in your bio, such as a link to your lead magnet.
▶ Post in the feed once per week (This can be from your business or personal page).
▶ Comment in relevant groups three times per week.

Additional Thoughts on Social Channels

You'll notice I'm talking a lot about LinkedIn. This may very well be where the majority of your business comes from. Of course, this varies by industry and individual, but it's important to keep in mind. After all, people who are seeking your consulting assistance are also professionals, and LinkedIn is where they gather online. If you're strapped for time, just focus on LinkedIn. As you start to see real results from any platform (meaning leads and conversions), you can increase the amount of time and content produced.

You also need to quantify the value of each channel with real key performance indicators (KPIs). You can get a bunch of likes by posting a funny meme, but that's probably not going to generate any revenue. Take a look at your Google Analytics to determine how many visits you're getting from specific social channels and what actions they're taking once they arrive. It's a simple report that will help you better understand the real impact of your social media presence and lead to strategic content creation.

Here are the steps involved:

- ▶ Install Google Analytics.
- ▶ Select "All Traffic."
- ▶ Under "Default Channel Grouping," look for "Social."
- ▶ Click the hyperlink for "Social."

You'll now be able to see how much traffic and conversions you're getting from each Social channel. Please note, this involves tracking conversions (such as a form submission), which I highly recommend.

This part can seem a bit confusing, but it's worth putting in the effort so you can learn how to manage and interpret this data. I suggest taking the free training offered by the Google Analytics Academy (https://analytics.google.com/analytics/academy/). This will take you around three hours, but you'll have a better understanding of your impact from social media and any other traffic source. For example, you'll be able to see how much organic traffic you're attracting with those blogs you've been writing.

This attribution and accountability are key to optimizing any of your online efforts.

Why This Is Important

Not only is social media a great way for you to connect with potential clients and business partners, it's also an excellent way to showcase your personality alongside the value you have to offer.

You can also use it to keep a pulse on what's going on with your audience so you can be aware of any relevant updates or events. You won't find an easier way to continuously perform audience research.

Action Items

- ▶ Determine if you want to build the website yourself or hire a professional.
- ▶ Write copy for your website homepage and About section.
- ▶ Determine ten questions your audience has, and create content that answers these questions.
- ▶ Get feedback, and make adjustments as needed.
- ▶ Determine your username, and set up social media accounts.
- ▶ Determine how often you would like to initially post—start off slow.
- ▶ Repurpose blog content as social media posts.
- ▶ Identify relevant LinkedIn groups to join.
- ▶ Practice writing cold outreach messages.
- ▶ Learn how to report on social media traffic in Google Analytics.

Activating
and Growing
Your Network

"Your network is your net worth." I'm sure this quote is familiar to many of you. While it may not be 100 percent accurate, developing and leveraging your network can greatly fast-track your success. Here's a brief story to help illustrate that.

I met Howie See while attending college at the University at Buffalo. We both worked at the same bar. He was a DJ; I checked IDs at the door. Since he was a DJ at the most popular bar on campus, Howie knew a ton of people. He was also incredibly nice, which helped him make genuine connections with people.

After school, he was working in wealth management in multiple companies in New York, then moved to Los Angeles and worked for a friend to try to grow their business. He then decided to go a different direction using his experience to offer advanced strategy to all businesses, no matter the size. Providing consultative CTO and IT director services, he advises on technology strategies, project manages moves or buildouts, and audits existing businesses and potential acquisitions.

Although he was from New York, the social skills he developed helped him quickly grow his network in Los Angeles. In fact, this is how he got his first client. Howie recalls,

> *My first client was introduced to me through one of the clients I worked with when I was at my previous company. It was an ultra-high-profile client, and for them to recommend me was quite amazing. I was just worried about the part of business I really hated: accounting, invoicing, expense tracking, and all of the legal/tax law that I needed to now somehow understand.*

When asked about the transformation he states: "I realize today, it was the best choice I've made for me, and my current and previous clients. The first six months going solo was frightening but also very exciting. I fortunately had just signed a new client and had them on a retainer, which made the transition easier."

Unlike most of the other consultants referenced, Howie doesn't have a positioning statement, and it's by design. "I am sort of a black book for all of my clients. Whatever you need, I probably know someone who can help you with that. I find many inefficiencies with most businesses that translate into hidden costs. I am your almost one-stop shop for all things business."

Howie's story is a perfect example of how your network can help grow your business, no matter how niche it may be.

Meg McKeen shares another example: "My first client was a former client during a corporate role; we developed great rapport over the years, and when I embarked on this project, he was gracious to continue supporting me by retaining me to train one of his new salespeople."

Like Meg, Natalie Allport's first client came from a former business partnership. "My first client was one of my sponsors when I was an athlete! They were a family-owned sporting store chain, and I was definitely nervous about it. Having this prior, more personal relationship with the client made the pressure higher as I did not want to disappoint them or ruin the relationship. This pushed me to learn and grow fast, and I am proud to have worked with this client for over six years now!"

Jake Savage managed to land his first client through a current business partnership at the full-time job he held while transitioning to becoming an independent consultant.

My first client was actually a client of the company I worked for prior to becoming a full-time consultant. Both the founder and VP of sales (of my first client) followed me on social media and had become consumers of my sales content. When their HR team mentioned that they were looking to hire an outside sales trainer, my name was recommended! This company is not a small fish so I was pretty shocked to hear that they had selected me to be their trainer. Their budget easily could've supported any big-name consultant. I was pretty nervous going into it!

Irene Papajohn landed her first client through a friend from college.

My first client came through a classmate. One of his friends needed someone who could wear many hats in the marketing space. He sent an email introducing us, and that conversation led to a project and a relationship that has lasted two years and counting. I was honestly just trying to understand what they needed and if I was a good fit. I really didn't have any expectations for the conversation.

Amina AlTai was able to book her first project just by openly communicating with her network. "My first clients came through my community. I was sharing about my career evolution with friends and colleagues, and they became my best referral sources."

Anna Vatuone has a similar story about how she got her first client. "It was through a friend of a friend. I couldn't believe someone was ACTUALLY willing to pay me for my expertise. I was so nervous."

I bring all this up to highlight the fact that you most likely either already know your first client, or you know someone who can connect you to them. You just have to make them aware of what you're doing and how they can help.

Now that your online presence is set up, you're ready to launch. Things are about to get real, and it can be a bit scary. Fortunately, you're not in it alone. There are dozens, maybe even hundreds of people who would be happy to help. This chapter walks through how to reposition yourself, introduce your new company, and actively seek work or referrals.

Tina has already reached out to numerous friends and former colleagues for feedback. In addition to offering their input, the majority have also asked how they can help spread the word on her behalf. Although she did her best to empower them, Tina didn't have a formal approach in place. We're going to work on that shortly.

The Reintroduction Letter

If you ask most people in your network what you do for work, they probably have a loose understanding. You're about to change all that with your reintroduction letter. This is your opportunity to inform them of the pivot you've made and enlist their help in growing your new business. The easier you make it for them to help, the better. This means clearly describing:

▶ What you do
▶ Who you do it for
▶ How they can help

Now, before you start sending out these emails, you'll want to organize and prioritize. When possible, a more personalized email is preferable, but that may be extremely time consuming depending on the size of your network.

Sort your list in the following way.

If you offer services to individuals. People who may want your service. They should be your top priority, so make it personal. Put some thought into how you'll start off your email. Reference anything new they have going on and/or ask a genuine question. This may involve some research on your part. People who may be connected to others who want your service. This may be the majority of your personal network. If you're short on time, it's OK to go a bit broader with this audience. Start off by saying something like, "Hope all is well on your end," then cut to the chase. Don't phone it in, but don't spend hours researching their Instagram feed just to find something to talk about.

If you offer services to organizations. People who work at organizations that may want your service and have purchasing power. Again, this is top priority. If you can go straight to the top, you'll greatly accelerate the process of getting an opportunity to describe your services. If you know them well, ask for an in-person meeting to catch up, but also reference your availability for a phone call. People who work at organizations that may want your service and can influence decisions. While these individuals still provide value, it may be more challenging for them to help, especially if they work at a larger organization. That said, you never know where they'll go next—either within their organization or elsewhere, so you'll definitely want to connect with them.

Here's the reintroduction letter I sent my network once I started helping other consultants as opposed to focusing on digital marketing.

Subject: All Me to Reintroduce Myself

Hi [Name]

Hope your New Year is off to a great start!

I'm reaching out to make you aware of some updates on my end.

For years, I've primarily helped organizations and individuals as a digital marketer. While I enjoyed doing this, I'm now more passionate about teaching other entrepreneurs how to generate revenue through consulting, speaking engagements, and other knowledge-based opportunities. In short, I now coach other consultants.

As you may have guessed, I'm about to ask for your help!

I'm wondering if you or anyone in your network would be interested in learning more about the services I provide. You can get more information on my website. But to summarize, I help consultants clarify the value they provide a specific audience and then attract opportunities that will pay them what they're worth for this knowledge.

I've enjoyed working with the following types of entrepreneurs:

- ▶ Consultants

- ▶ Workshop leaders

- ▶ Online course creators

- ▶ Agency owners

Another way you can help would be to introduce me to organizations (such as a local college or entrepreneur organization) that would be open to having me speak to their community. You can get all the information you would need to spread the word on this Google doc.

Thanks for your support! If you'd like to schedule a call with me—whether you're interested in my services or just want to catch up—you can do so here. Outside of that, don't hesitate to reach out with any questions, and let me know if there's anything I can do to support you as well.

Best,

Terry

Let's break down what I did here.

I started off with a warm but vague hello. People know I tend to get to the point quickly, so there's no need to string this out. For all I know, they're reading this on their cell phone and I want to qualify their time. I then let them know what I'm up to and how they can help. Providing specifics on the types of people or opportunities you're interested in is key. This is why I listed use cases from people I've already worked with. In your case, you may not have any clients yet, but that's totally fine. Just make them aware of your target audience.

Here's one of the most important things I did: I created a Google doc that provided additional information, which I'll share shortly. Why? I need to make it as easy as possible for them to spread the word. My goal is to reduce the friction involved with getting them to help. Asking them to summarize what I've said *and* share it with their network increases this friction.

Here's the additional information I provided.

Document title: Terry Rice Consulting

Thanks for your willingness to spread the word about my business. To make things easier, I've summarized my services and provided a template for you to share this information with your network and/or decision makers at your organization.

Hi [Name]

I'm reaching out in regard to your consulting service. I've known Terry Rice for quite some time and I recently found out he coaches other consultants just like you. I've included his bio below.

In short, he helps consultants clarify the value they provide a specific audience, and then attract opportunities that will pay them what they're worth for this knowledge. You can get more details on his website.

Would you like me to make an introduction? Or feel free to reach out to him directly at terry@terryrice.co

Best,

Jessica

Terry Rice is a business development consultant based in Brooklyn. As the founder of Terry Rice Consulting, he helps entrepreneurs monetize their knowledge without sacrificing their health, family, or personal interests. His focus is advising professionals on how to launch or scale their knowledge-based businesses, which can include consulting, speaking appearances, online courses, and associated revenue streams. Terry is also an adjunct instructor at NYU where he leads workshops for career-driven individuals. A recognized digital marketing expert, his previous experience includes helping clients achieve their business goals while working at Adobe and Facebook.

This is short by design. It gives the sender the freedom to add more information if they'd like, while not requiring it. Adding the bio is a nice touch because they may choose to include or repurpose it in some other way.

A question that comes up often is: Why am I sharing this additional information as a Google Doc? Why not include it in my original email, or give a link to my website with this same information?

There are a few reasons:

- ▶ If I include all this information in the email, it will make it way too long.
- ▶ I could include this information on my website, but someone might accidentally stumble upon it as a result of SEO.
- ▶ Opening a PDF on your mobile phone involves downloading, and it's also harder to copy and paste.
- ▶ Google Docs are dynamic. If I want to change the text provided, I can do so without sending out a new email to everyone.

I know this outreach can be challenging. You may feel like you're bugging people or you're afraid people will think you're desperate. The sooner you get over that feeling, the sooner you can start bringing in your first clients. Some people may judge you, but then they'll just go about the rest of their day. Others will simply ignore you, and that's OK, too. You never know what they have going on in their life. You just need a few people to take action and you'll be well on your way to engaging with prospects who are already excited to speak with you.

Don't skip this exercise. If you don't have a contact's email address, reach out to them on social media with a more truncated message. The Google Doc you created will certainly come in handy here. As usual, track all results in your CRM so you can see the source of the leads you'll generate. Also, be sure to say thanks to anyone who responds, whether they can help you or not.

Action Items

- ▶ Create a list of people who may want your services and a separate list of people who may be able to recommend your services.
- ▶ Draft a reintroduction letter, providing them with all necessary information.

▶ Track responses in your CRM.

▶ Say thanks to anyone who responded, and consider sending a small gift to anyone who helped you land a meeting or client.

9

Getting in Front of Your Target Audience

(Passive Prospecting)

W hen I first started my consulting business, I often gave free lunch-and-learn sessions at various coworking spaces in New York City. My most popular sessions included "Facebook Advertising for Founders," "How to Generate Leads on Social Media," and "Search Engine Optimization for Local Businesses."

I spent hours creating and editing these presentations. I was initially afraid I wouldn't have enough content or wouldn't deliver enough value. I was somewhat anxious when presenting, too. I soon discovered there was no reason to be nervous. Everyone is there to learn from you, so they want you to do well. You have an audience of allies—not adversaries—in front of you. I also found out you should expect a lot of questions, so you'll most likely have too much content as opposed to the other way around!

Over time, I could easily deliver these presentations with no prep required. I could focus on being who I was, which allowed me to deliver even more value.

Getting in front of your target audience is one of the most effective ways to land new clients. You may very well land your first clients by activating your network, but you'll need to get used to making these connections yourself. Without numerous references or years in business, it can be challenging for people to trust you. However, it's easier to build trust through face-to-face interaction. In this chapter, we'll dive into strategies to get you in front of your audience and build a following.

It all starts with having something to say, which is why we'll begin this chapter with a discussion about developing your signature speaking topics.

Signature Speaking Topics

The majority of professional speakers are known for a handful of specific speeches they can deliver. These are known as their signature speeches. This is what they're passionate and knowledgeable about. Unknowingly, I followed the same approach when delivering my lunch-and-learns.

Often, event organizers don't want a custom presentation; they want your best presentation. It reduces the risk involved, and they know exactly what the audience will get out of it, because it's a proven entity that you've perfected over time. You can use this same approach to develop your own signature speaking topics. Establishing these will be your fast-track to getting booked to speak at relevant events, both online and in person.

When developing your speaking topic, you need to focus on the following:

▶ *Your audience.* Who are they? What do you think their goals are? How can you provide value?

▶ *Your title.* If your audience saw a magazine with your presentation title on the cover, what would make them pick it up to learn more? How can you craft a title that will draw in attendees?

▶ *The problem you're solving or the action you're encouraging.* What is the "why" of your presentation? What are you going to do for the attendees?

▶ *Key takeaways or next steps.* How can you set up attendees for success once they've left your presentation? What are the actionable items they can take from you?

You can create a road map like this for every presentation you have in your repertoire. Here's the outline from my own Facebook session:

Facebook Advertising for Founders

Everyone says Facebook is an easy way to target and engage with your target audience. Unfortunately, they didn't mention how challenging it can be to figure out how to use the platform in the first place. As a founder, you wear many hats but need to focus on impact. During this session, we'll cover the need to know aspects of Facebook marketing. By the end, you'll be able to determine whether you want to take this on yourself or delegate to someone else.

Key Takeaways:

▶ Learn the anatomy of a successful Facebook campaign.

▶ Find out how to interpret key success metrics to drive decision making.

▶ Discover how to track and optimize your budget.

▶ Determine how or if you can best leverage the platform.

You can find more examples by looking at workshop descriptions from other organizations. The key is to make very clear what you have to offer, and identify the transformation your audience can expect.

It's beneficial to develop three signature topics that you can craft a presentation around. You can then list them on your website and have a menu for organizers to choose from. Keep these short—one hour, tops. You can always make it shorter or longer if needed. Also, be sure to include storytelling, even if you're not referencing work you've done.

Local Places to Speak

Now that you have your topics prepared, you can start pitching them to relevant organizations. Let's walk through a few common local venues that often welcome guest presenters.

Coworking Spaces

Shared working spaces are always looking for ways to provide more value to their members. If you can deliver information that will help the community members grow their businesses or improve their personal lives, you're in a great position to land a speaking opportunity.

Do some research first. Do these organizations typically bring in guest speakers? If so, what topics do they usually present on? If you can find a detailed session description from past presentations, you can mirror that approach in your outreach.

If it doesn't appear they've led events like this in the past, you may have to justify that in your pitch. I did so by describing how my event would not only bring value to their current members but how they could also use it as a marketing tactic to bring in potential other members by making my event open to the public. Try this approach. By doing so, you can position yourself as a way to enhance their community and generate leads. You can go from being a random person sending them an email to a potential business partner. Here is a sample outreach email that will help you pitch your presentation:

Subject line: Quick Question

Body:

Hi Joey,

I was wondering if you ever brought in speakers to lead sessions at your office. I have a few prepared talks about digital marketing I believe your members could benefit from. This is also an opportunity for you to get more prospects at your office by providing a tour before I get started.

Is this something you'd be interested in chatting about? You can book a time here, but don't hesitate to reach out with additional questions via email as well.

Best,

Terry

terryrice.co/speaking

As you can see, there is no need to get super wordy in your outreach email. Just provide enough information to pique their interest. If you can land a speaking opportunity at an organization that has multiple locations, you're in luck. You can then ask that organizer to introduce you to others in your area or a regional director. You could be well on your way to delivering multiple presentations in a very short period of time, which can easily lead to landing more clients. You'll also get better at delivering your content because you can make adjustments and start including commonly asked questions.

I once spoke at WeWork labs and was quickly introduced to the regional director who connected me with five other WeWork labs in New York City. The same could easily happen for you.

Chambers of Commerce

If you joined your local chamber of commerce, speaking to local chapters should be a viable opportunity for you. However, you may have to wait a bit depending on the demand.

I suggest attending events that are similar to the one you want to lead so you can get a feel for the atmosphere and flow. Afterward, speak to the person who led the event. Thank them for their time and ask to connect in the future. This will be a great way for you to learn more about them and how they landed the opportunity to speak. If the event organizer was present, you'll want to speak directly to them as well. If this isn't an option, send them an email explaining how you've attended events in the past, and would love to host one as well.

If they agree, ask if you can provide some sort of discount or freebie for anyone who attends. Chambers enjoy being able to provide their members with perks because it increases the sense of community and justifies the cost of membership. Although you want to be cautious about discounting your fees, doing so is well justified in this situation. Here's why: If you can land a client who is a member of your chamber (and do a good job in your presentation), word of your expertise will quickly spread among other members. You'll have people walking up to you at the next event asking about your services. You've already established the trust and credibility required to attract the right clients. This could all happen in just a matter of months.

Speaking at Meetups

Browse the groups on www.Meetup.com, a site that helps you meet groups of people in your area based on common interests, or similar sites. If you find one that would be a good fit for your target audience, consider reaching out to see if they ever bring in guest speakers. I followed this approach and was able to speak at several Meetups that catered to entrepreneurs or small businesses. Again, my signature topics came in handy here, but I usually had to deliver a much shorter version.

Similar to the chamber of commerce, this could be a relatively tight-knit group. If you can land one of them as a client, they'll spread the word to other groups and organizations. For this reason, I also suggest offering a discount or freebie. Here's the big difference. though: You don't want to pitch yourself in a way that seems salesy or cheesy. Consider attending one or two events before inquiring about speaking there. Your pitch email would be similar to the one you wrote for the coworking space.

Subject line: Quick Question

Body:

Hi Joey,

I've attended a few of your meetings. I've enjoyed both the information presented and the community you've created.

I was wondering if you ever brought in speakers to lead sessions at your meetings. I have a few prepared talks about digital marketing I believe your members could benefit from. I can deliver the presentation in as little as 15 minutes.

Is this something you'd be interested in chatting about? You can book a time here, but don't hesitate to reach out with additional questions via email as well.

Best,

Terry

terryrice.co/speaking

Notice, I stated how quickly I could deliver the content. This goes a long way in reducing the friction involved with getting a yes. As always, if you're able to inquire about speaking while you're at an event, this can greatly accelerate the process.

Local Colleges or Other Educational Institutions

Teaching at a recognized educational institution is an incredibly valuable way to fast-track your credibility and lead generation. Imagine what it will feel like to just show up and already have a room full of people waiting to hear what you have to say. Not only that, but you'll be also able to experience this consistently, without the need to handle any of the marketing or logistics that got the attendees there. The big benefit to speaking at a college or university is that they will do the event marketing for you.

Teaching at General Assembly was pivotal to my success as a consultant. At times, I was teaching up to three classes a week with a total of around 60 students. These weren't just students—they were local professionals who wanted to enhance their current skills or develop entirely new ones. Not only that, but they also already invested in their education by attending my class. Anytime you can get in front of people who understand the need to financially invest in their personal or professional development, it's going to be much easier to sell your services.

You're often better off speaking to 20 people who paid $99 to attend a class as opposed to 200 people who came to a free event. This has certainly been my experience.

As you can imagine, this approach to growing your reputation and landing clients can be competitive, so you'll have to work extra hard to stand out. I applied to General Assembly several times without receiving any real response. Eventually, I posted a message on WeWork's internal communications platform asking for help. Another member saw my message, connected me with a recruiter from General Assembly, and I was on my way. You might have to find a more creative way to make a connection too. It will be worth it.

One challenge you may run into when pitching to colleges and universities is lack of teaching experience. If you were a teacher's assistant or something similar in college, be sure to mention that in the application. If not, you'll want to speak to the workshops you've led at other organizations. Keep in mind, these can be any workshops you may have led, not just the ones you've done as an independent consultant. If you have testimonials, now is a good time to surface them.

Securing an opportunity as a guest speaker for a class is much easier than securing a formal teaching role, so this may be a great place for you to start. In this case, there may not be an application form readily available, so you'll need to send an email to the instructor and/or the facility.

Subject line: Quick Question

Body:

Hi Dr. Smith,

I was wondering if you ever brought in guest speakers to lead sessions during your classes. I have a few prepared talks about digital marketing I believe your students could benefit from. I've led similar sessions for professionals at various locations in the area.

Is this something you'd be interested in chatting with? You can book a time here, but don't hesitate to reach out with additional questions via email as well.

Best,

Terry

terryrice.co/speaking

Notice I'm emphasizing the fact I've already taught this content in the past. You can include this while contacting other organizations as well, but it's imperative to do this if you want to speak at an educational institution. If you know what specific classes or areas of concentration you would be a good fit for, be sure to mention that. If possible, contact the person who manages the curriculum or staffing for these classes.

In many cases, they'll ask you to do a sample teaching lesson. If you get this far, there's a good chance you'll land the opportunity!

Local Conferences

I've spoken at conferences with roughly 20 attendees, total. Sure, it wasn't a huge stage, but these opportunities can still be extremely valuable, so long as you're speaking to your target audience. You may still connect with some potential clients and you'll continue building your brand locally. As you can imagine, it's also much easier to get your foot in the door at these smaller conferences as opposed to a larger event. You most likely won't get paid, but you'll be able to get pictures of yourself talking to a crowd. It may even be worth hiring your own videographer to record if the organizers allow it.

If the event doesn't have a formal speaker application, I suggest reaching out with the following:

Subject line: Speaking at Brooklyn Entrepreneurs Conference

Body:

Hi Joey,

I was wondering if you're still looking for speakers for the upcoming Brooklyn Entrepreneurs conference. I have a few prepared talks about digital marketing I believe your attendees could benefit from. I've led similar sessions for professionals at various locations in the area.

Is this something you'd be interested in chatting with? You can book a time here, but don't hesitate to reach out with additional questions via email as well.

Best,

Terry

terryrice.co/speaking

In this case, I made it crystal clear why I was reaching out in the subject line. There is no need to beat around the bush with this particular audience—they are expecting people to reach out and need to fill a roster of speakers.

Best Practices for Presentations

Just getting in front your audience will be beneficial, but you'll do even better if you actively encourage the next steps.

▶ *Make it very clear people can hire you.* When I first started teaching at General Assembly, I didn't overtly say, "This is what I do for a living." Instead, I simply provided my email address and encouraged people to reach out if they had any questions. At the advice of a friend, I added a slight call to action. I simply said, "Also available for company and individual training" in addition to my contact information. That's it. All of sudden, about 20 percent of people who attended my sessions started reaching out for individual consulting and a large percentage converted to clients. These were usually shorter-term engagements, but it's clearly more than I would have received if I said nothing.

▶ *Provide your deck in exchange for their email address.* You'll notice people are frantically taking notes or snapping pictures of every slide. That's a good thing! Offer your deck in exchange for their email address. Create a landing page on your website where they can submit this information. I suggest making a Bit.ly link that is somewhat aligned with the event they're attending to make it easy to remember. So, for Brooklyn Entrepreneurs Conference, I could make it bit.ly/ricebec, which is my last name and the first letter of every word in the title of the event.

▶ *Make a slide that references the Bit.ly link and encourage people to take a picture of it.* Do this at the beginning and end of your presentation. They may not have been interested at first, but you can easily win them over after you deliver compelling content.

To capture the contact information you need, include the following fields in the form they'll fill out:

▶ Name
▶ Email address
▶ Are you interested learning more about my consulting services (Checkbox "Yes" "No, thanks"
▶ Message (optional)

Asking if someone is interested in working with you is an excellent filter to put in place. The next day (or maybe the same day) you'll reach out to them and set up an enrollment conversation. Following this process will help you connect with them while they're still excited about your presentation so you can keep the momentum going.

Here's a template for your follow-up email.

Title: Brooklyn Entrepreneurs Conference Follow-Up

Hi Joey,

Thanks for attending my session yesterday. I had a great time engaging with all of you.

I appreciate your interest in learning more about my services. In short, I help entrepreneurs like you determine how to best scale their budget and resources on various digital marketing channels.

I'd like to learn more about you and the goals you have for your organization. You can book a discovery call with me here. However, please let me know if you need any additional availability.

I look forward to speaking with you shortly, but don't hesitate to reach out with any questions during the interim.

Best,

Terry

terryrice.co

▶ *Come up with an excuse for them to go to your website.* Your deck may be enough to get some people to submit their email address, but you may have to provide more concrete or specific value to get other attendees interested. This is where your lead magnet can come in handy. Mention it a few times, then provide a Bit.ly link for it or mention the fact that it's on your homepage. If you have other resources that would be a good fit for this audience, mention that as well.

▶ *Add a link to your online scheduling platform.* If the audience largely comprises people you'd like to work with, consider putting up a link to your online scheduling program. You can say something like, "I know questions are going to come up after the session. You're all welcome to book a 20-minute discovery call with me, even if you never plan on using my services." It might sound counterintuitive to potentially turn this enrollment call into a "pick my brain" session, but this approach will be beneficial. You'll get a chance to enroll some attendees, and you'll learn a lot just from talking to the others. As you're just starting out, these "pick my brain" sessions will provide you with a great deal of information and experience you can leverage as your business grows. Your empathy map will become more robust, and you'll get more comfortable talking to your audience.

▶ *Encourage people to take pictures.* Getting pictures of yourself in front of a crowd will go a long way in building your credibility. It will also make it easier to get more event opportunities going forward. At the beginning of your presentation, say something like, "I love collecting pictures from these events. If you take any, can you please share them with me via email, or tag me on social?" You may feel awkward about asking this at first, but don't let that hold you back. People will either ignore you or oblige you. In my experience, just asking this question encourages people to take even more pictures. If they tag you on social, share their posts as quickly as possible, and thank them for doing so. Following this process will allow you to amplify the impact of speaking at any event. You may even be able to add some of the pictures to your website.

▶ *Post about the event on social media within the next few days.* This is your chance to continue amplifying the impact of your event appearance. If you have photos, now is the time to share. Of course, you'll want to provide some context as well. Don't say, "I had a great time speaking at . . ." and just leave it at that. This can easily come off as bragging if you don't provide value in exchange for the audience's attention. I strongly suggest mentioning a few takeaways from your talk, and asking others to comment with their thoughts as well. You'll get a lot more engagement and create an opportunity to have a conversation as opposed to just talking about yourself.

Here's an example of text you could include with a photo:

Yesterday I presented at the Brooklyn Entrepreneurs Conference. We discussed the best ways to take advantage of social media, even when you're strapped for time. Leveraging Instagram Stories was a popular choice since they require far less creative development. How do you manage to create content while balancing out other responsibilities?

You're still spreading the word about speaking at an event, but you're doing so in a way that provides more value and encourages interaction.

▶ *Play the long game.* Although I expect you to gain immediate traction from these events, you'll also want to exercise patience. Realize that some things take time to unfold and you may not book enrollment calls with people who seem like the perfect fit. Don't radically change your approach to be more salesy, just understand this is all part of the process. I often get contacted by people who heard me speak somewhere years ago—I'm surprised they even remember me. These prospects usually convert a lot quicker because they've had to think about who they want to partner with and they chose me. You're going to experience this as well. For years, you'll get emails and LinkedIn messages from people saying that met you at some random event and would love to chat with you further. You probably won't remember most of them, but they'll remember you. Like the saying goes, people will forget what you did, but people will never forget how you made them feel. So, don't make them feel like you're a cheesy used car salesman who's just trying to make a buck!

Why This Is Important

Your signature speaking topics are the key to creating relationships with organizations who can get you in front of a large audience. Instead of spending time trying to get one individual to pay attention to you on social media, you can get in front of several without the need to promote yourself in advance.

Beyond being a sought-after attendee, you'll also learn a great deal from the questions and conversations that come up during the event. Of course, your attendance is also something you can eventually charge for, providing you with an opportunity to get paid to prospect!

Action Items

- ▶ Develop your first signature speaking topic.
- ▶ Determine areas where you can present in person. If available, look for an event calendar on their site to get a feel for who they usually bring in.
- ▶ Leverage your outreach templates to connect with organizers.
- ▶ Consider adding a "Speaking" page to your website.
- ▶ If applicable, apply for an instructor position at a local educational institution.

Sales and Marketing

This part can be intimidating, even for the most experienced consultant. Nobody wants to feel like they're bothering someone or come off as pushy. The best way to address this is to provide value in exchange for your audience's attention so they proactively reach out to you for help. You'll do this through the content you create and the partnerships you develop. For example, Meg McKeen typically lands clients through a combination of both of these approaches.

> *My network in insurance is deep; it's a 'big, small world,' so many conversations are extensions of those that have started years ago. LinkedIn has been a total gift in the development of my broader network; having a platform that allows you to tell your story in your own voice and connect authentically with individuals around the globe who need what you have to offer is perhaps the greatest tool available to those new in business.*

Natalie Allport generates the majority of her leads through word-of-mouth and organic social media. If you follow her on Instagram @natalieallport, you'll notice she interviews people her audience can identify with on a regular basis. This is an approach you may want to consider as well. It will allow you to quickly crank out high-quality content while also building your personal brand. Please note, you don't have to interview "celebrities." Start with people who you can access and will resonate with your target audience.

Jake Savage leverages LinkedIn and his podcast to attract leads. Although podcasts are clearly an audio form of communication, he videotapes all the episodes so he can repurpose the content on social media. Another approach you may want to consider is interviewing people with whom you may want to work. This provides you with a value-added reason to initially connect with them, which could eventually lead to a business relationship.

Kellen Driscoll takes a more traditional approach:

> *I do a lot out outreach to my existing network via email and phone. While I do this, I am not asking them directly if they want my coaching. I am asking who they know that needs my coaching. Many times this turns into, 'Hey, I need your coaching.' Other times, they may refer another person or another company. Or often, they may not even respond!*

Not one to be discouraged, Kellen continues his outreach with an additional approach: "I offer my services to numerous other coaches and consultants as an add-on to their offering. I just do this via direct outreach, or they will come in via a referral from my existing network." It's worth considering how you could attach your services to another provider. If you make the right connection, you'll have opportunities show up out of nowhere. This largely eliminates the need to do any marketing or presales, leaving you to focus on providing value.

Of course, you need to get clients to get referrals! Mike Swigunski provides a great approach as you're just starting out. "I get a large number of leads by creating quality content, which involves promoting via YouTube, Facebook groups, and other social media channels. From there, I present my lead magnet as a natural way to capture contact information." Again, this is why it's so important to develop your lead magnet, especially in the early stages of your business.

In time, you'll be more concerned with deciding who *you* want to work with as opposed to worry about who wants to work with you.

After speaking at her chamber of commerce, Tina was able to land a few solid leads, which she quickly documented in her CRM. However, she realized there was a finite number of in-person activities she could do every month and also wanted to expand her service area. She decided it was time to expand the scope of her business development by performing both inbound and outbound marketing. The idea behind inbound marketing is to create and distribute relevant and valuable content that the customers want. They may discover it on social media, while performing a Google search, or by catching your video on YouTube. Outbound marketing includes proactive approaches such as cold email marketing, paid ads, and direct messaging on social media.

Getting in front of your audience is one of the best ways to generate leads and eventually win business. However, you'll also need to develop a more robust business development strategy. You'll need to actively connect with prospects who may not be overly familiar with you, let them know you understand their problem, and provide a solution. In this chapter, we'll cover how to do so in a way that doesn't feel salesy or desperate.

Video Content

Creating video content is a great way to provide value while showing your personality at the same time. Don't worry if you feel like someone else has already made a video on the exact same topic; your personality will be the unique differentiator. Also, realize it may take some time getting used to being on camera. That's fine; it's all part of your personal and professional development process. But you can't skip that part. When you're creating videos, it's helpful to imagine you're talking to one specific person. This will help you feel more relaxed and present yourself in a more authentic way.

In time, you'll be pleased and surprised by people who reach out saying, "You know, I saw your video, and it's clear you really understand what I'm going through."

YouTube

YouTube is the world's second largest search engine. Your audience is most likely on there looking for answers to their questions. As we've discussed, questions create content. You can easily provide value and get discovered by creating video content that answers these questions.

The thought of being on camera may be scary. Before you decide to skip this part, though, search YouTube for at least one of the ten questions your audience has. You'll pull this from the same list you previously made. Now, look at a few of the videos that come up in your search. Sure, some of them will be highly produced with a great background and fantastic lighting, but you'll see others that have far less production value involved. It could be as simple as someone sharing their screen. Now, take a look at the comments. You'll notice viewers are still getting value from this content. You don't need 100,000 views to be successful; a few hundred views from the right audience will still go a long way in establishing your expertise and exposing you to new people.

If you really want to nail this, take a look at the comments from the videos you're researching. You'll discover what people like, and don't like, about the content presented. While you should not copy anyone, you should obviously take note on how their audience reacts.

Also, keep in mind that producing quality video is a skill that takes time to develop. Most likely, your first video won't be that great, but your tenth video will be much better. Like many things in life, you can't skip the part where you figure stuff out. However, you can make it easier by studying people who appear to be doing well in your niche.

I suggest starting with a brief Instagram Story video. Stories have a 60-second time cap and they disappear after 24 hours. Once you get more comfortable, create YouTube videos that answer the list of ten questions you previously developed. Be sure to include the question in the title of your video, and provide links back to your website.

LinkedIn

While YouTube is a great platform, it also relies on people searching for your content. For this reason, I strongly suggest creating video content that is more tailored to LinkedIn. Your videos will show up in the News Feed as opposed to people searching for it. Typically, your videos created for LinkedIn should be much shorter in duration. While the maximum length of a LinkedIn video is currently ten minutes, try to keep yours under the three-minute mark to keep your viewer engaged. Also, be sure to upload a video directly to the platform; don't post a link to YouTube. If you post natively, your video will auto-play in the News Feed, which will give you more visibility and reach. Include an engaging and descriptive text headline that will encourage viewers to watch. For example, "In this video I break down the five most common roadblocks that are preventing you from getting more sleep." As always, be sure to use relevant hashtags and encourage viewers to interact.

Beyond that, you can also include a link to your LinkedIn video in any prospecting messages you send. Again, this will auto-play in the recipient's inbox. This part is important. You'll now have the ability to provide value and show your personality while prospecting. Keep this video super short—less than 30 seconds if possible.

Explainer Videos

You can also start creating explainer videos to post on your own site and various other channels such as YouTube and LinkedIn. As the name suggests, this involves explaining concepts or tools to your audience. For example, I use Acuity for scheduling my enrollment calls, so I made an explainer video showing other consultants how they can do the same. Sure, Acuity already has this content available, but my personality and the way I describe use cases will be the differentiator. You can do the same thing. These explainer videos also come in handy when you're speaking at events. You can simply say, "I have an explainer video about this, which you can view by going to my YouTube channel." Again, this means there will be more eyeballs on your content, and you can provide value without getting into the weeds of a complicated topic. An unintended (or intended) bonus of creating these explainer videos is that you can include affiliate links for some of the products or services you mention. We'll get into affiliate marketing in detail later in Chapter 14. For now, just note that it's a way to get paid to promote another company's products or services. Acuity currently offers up to $30 if someone signs up for their platform using your affiliate link. With affiliate links, an explainer video you spent two hours creating could make you hundreds or thousands of dollars over the next several months.

I mention all the gear you'll need to get started with shooting video in the resources section of my website at www.terryrice.co/resources.

Free Webinars

Leading webinars on a regular basis means you always have an excuse to engage with a potential prospect. You'll be able to provide value in exchange for their attention. If you get into this rhythm, you may be able to land the majority of your clients without ever leaving your home or office.

This approach involves being on camera as well, except you'll get a chance to interact with your audience in real time. Leading free informational webinars is a great way to demonstrate your expertise without asking for prospects to make a financial commitment, or even leave their own home. You can go deeper on the ten questions from your list, or you can chat about anything else that would provide value like one of your signature speaking topics.

Once you determine your topic, you'll need to decide when to host this session. Of course, you want to get as many people to attend as possible. According to GoToMeeting (www.gotomeeting.com), Tuesday, Wednesday, and Thursday are the best days to schedule sessions like these. The 11 A.M. slot usually gets the highest percentage of registrants, and

2 P.M. comes in at a close second. As a rule, 11 A.M. to 2 P.M. are the best times to host a webinar. The only exception within that time frame is noon—it overlaps lunch hour. However, if you have attendees in multiple time zones, the best time for a webinar is 12 P.M. PST/3 P.M. EST. This involves breaking the lunch hour rule, but it's for the greater good.

I use Zoom for my webinars, and they've put together a handy list of best practices, which I've summarized and contributed to below. First, let's go over some best practices for your pre-event prep:

- ▶ *Make it clear you don't have to attend live.* No matter what day and time you schedule for, not everyone will be able to make it. Increase the number of signups by stating all registered attendees will get a copy of the deck and a recording of the session.
- ▶ *Create a brief but thorough registration form.* There is a risk of losing a percentage of your prospective attendees for each question you ask on your registration form. Stick with the need-to-know information such as their name, email, and one qualifying question. This question could be in regard to the industry they're in, asking for their website or even their position within a company. You should always ask for questions and comments and make that field optional.
- ▶ *Promote the event early and up to the start time.* Event promotion should start one month to two weeks prior to the event start date. Increase promotion frequency and tactics to include all viable channels as the date nears. You'll want to go heavy on LinkedIn. If you have an email list, be sure to make your subscribers aware as well.
- ▶ *Set your duration with care.* Webinars are typically one hour long. Keep in mind that attendees are in front of their computers—one of the most distracting environments ever. Even with a one-hour event, you should set aside at least ten minutes for interactive activity such as Q&A. If you need to deliver longer content, consider breaking up the session into multiple, bite-sized sections.

Next, let's talk about best practices for live events.

- ▶ *Use dual monitors.* It can be challenging to manage all aspects of an online event on a single monitor. Add screen sharing to that and you may find windows are always in your way while you present. With a second monitor, you can host the screen sharing on your primary display and move windows like your participants list, chat, and anything else to a secondary monitor. I often use the secondary monitor to look up participants' websites while they're chatting. Don't have dual monitors? Bring a second laptop, make sure it is made a co-host, and you can monitor additional features there.

▶ *Encourage a discussion-based presentation.* You obviously have content prepared, but your audience will get more bespoke input if they ask you questions. Start by asking people where they're from and what they do. Just make it clear you're not going to be talking to a computer screen for the next hour. If nobody responds, call on specific individuals. I often have a colleague or friend join just to make sure the conversation gets started. You'll find this gets others to begin contributing as well.

▶ *Make eye contact and be aware of your gestures.* Don't make the mistake of sharing slides the entire time. People showed up to talk to you! Talk to the camera and be aware of your gestures. Even if you're having challenges getting a slide to load or something along those lines, always appear to be in control and energetic. Simply smiling will maintain the positive atmosphere you've created.

▶ *Be sure to overtly mention next steps.* Now is the perfect time to book some enrollment calls. Make sure you have availability immediately after the call and for the next few days. Post a link to your scheduling platform multiple times during the session, and reinforce your availability at the end. You'll be amazed at how quickly your calendar fills up.

Finally, let's go over some post-event best practices:

▶ *Send the webinar materials out as quickly as possible.* Time kills deals, so get this information in attendees' hands fast. This will especially be important for the people who couldn't attend live. In your email, you'll again reinforce your availability for discovery calls and any other next steps that would be appropriate.

▶ *Ask for feedback.* This is your chance to improve, and maybe score a testimonial to promote your next webinar. Of course, you'll want to ask for permission first.

▶ *Provide a brief recap on social media.* You'll follow the same process we discussed with live events you spoke at. If any participants raved about the webinar, consider tagging them in the post. Something along the lines of "thanks for attending [name], [name], [name]" will do. They may see it and comment on your post. In addition to the social validation, this engagement will give you more reach in the news feed. I also suggest letting people know you can send them the deck and recording in exchange for their email address. You'll see an uptick in registrations, which could lead to more enrollment calls getting booked.

While leading webinars is a powerful way to capture the attention of your audience for an extended period of time, it does take effort to get registrations. For this reason, I strongly suggest aligning with other organization who already have access to a large audience, just like you did with your signature speaking topics. This will greatly reduce the amount of pressure (and perhaps anxiety) around getting people to attend, allowing you to focus more on developing and delivering valuable content. During the COVID shutdown, I was delivering two or three webinars per month on behalf of third parties. As a result, I was able to spend more time with my kids and less time focusing on business development. You have the same opportunity, so take advantage of it.

Appearing on Podcasts

This is by far one of my favorite ways to get in front of an audience. You can take advantage of the host's following, and it doesn't require any travel. During the conversation, you'll get to reveal your personality while also delivering value to an eager audience. You'll also get an opportunity to steer them toward your website and social channels.

Of course, you need to land these opportunities first. I've developed a four-step process you can easily implement and execute. Let's walk through it.

Identify the Podcasts You Want to Be On

This means finding the podcasts your target audience listens to. For me, this would include podcasts focusing on entrepreneurship. You can find the top-rated podcasts by topic on iTunes or similar platforms, but it will be extremely challenging to land an appearance on these more popular podcasts. Start off on a much smaller scale. Search by the category that makes sense, but you may have to scroll down for a while. You can also simply Google "topic + podcast" and see what comes up. This may be more useful if you're in a very niche field. I searched for "sustainable building materials podcast" and discovered *The Art of Construction,* a podcast that explores the world of construction with some of the best minds in the industry. If I consult on how to create buildings using sustainable products, this would obviously be a good fit for me. It doesn't matter if it's rated in the Top 100—my audience is listening to it.

If possible, I suggest having a virtual assistant create this list for you. It's going to be time consuming, and your efforts may be better spent elsewhere at this stage. You'll need the following information documented:

- ▶ Podcast title
- ▶ Podcast URL
- ▶ Host name
- ▶ Host social channels
- ▶ All available email address

Listen to the Podcast

So many people skip this step! Appearing on podcasts is a great way to build your brand, so you won't be the only one pitching yourself. Prove you're actually familiar with the host and theme by actually listening to a few episodes before reaching out. If appropriate, mention specific episodes in your outreach. You may also discover you don't want to be on the podcast for reason or another. You're better off finding out now as opposed to later.

I should note, you may be reaching out to hundreds of podcast hosts. If this is the case, only listen to the ones you really want to be on. If the other ones reply, you can vet them before agreeing to appear on the show.

Say Something Impactful

Assume the host is going to research you before responding. If you're not expressing a strong point of view or spreading relevant information, they may choose not to engage. Did something recently happen in your industry or area of concentration? Talk about it! If their audience is interested in it, and you're already talking about it, you put yourself in a great position to provide value.

Follow the Host on Social Media and Reach Out

You should be a student of the podcasts you hope to appear on and be ready with a purposeful pitch when it's time to reach out. Assuming this isn't a mass email, your message needs to reflect the fact that you've actually listened to the podcast and understand what type of content provides value to their audience. For example, Jason Feifer hosts a podcast called *Problem Solvers*. As per the website description, this podcast "features business owners and CEOs who went through a crippling business problem and came out the other side bigger and stronger. Feifer, *Entrepreneur's* editor in chief, pulls these stories out so other businesses can avoid the same crippling problems." Given this information, you can draft a more personalized email that looks like this:

> Hey Jason,
>
> I've enjoyed the inspirational and tactical-level information you and your guests share on *Problem Solvers*. At the end of your podcast, you note you're open to submissions from other entrepreneurs who are interested in appearing on the podcast. I'd like to tell you about a costly mistake that launched a multimillion dollar business.
>
> I used to make custom T-shirts, mostly for tourists in the Miami area. Five years ago I accidentally purchased 30 times the amount we usually stock. My credit

card had already been billed, so I had to find a way to sell these shirts quickly. At the time, my daughter was seven years old and heading off to her first year at summer camp in just a few months. I cringed at the thought of paying another bill, including the $30 for the shirts she had to wear at camp. That's when it hit me: we should be the T-shirt provider for her summer camp! I contacted the camp organizers and offered them a steep discount in exchange for their business. Fortunately, they said yes! I then reached out to 20 other summer camps and was able to sell through my inventory. I then decided to rebrand as Camps Tees. Last year we did $6 million in annual revenue, while also expanding to hats and shorts. Is this something you'd be interested in chatting with me about? You can book a time here, but don't hesitate to reach out with additional questions via email as well.

Best,

Terry

terryrice.co

This is an approach you could use if you're pitching a more competitive podcast. For podcasts with a smaller audience, the same approach used when pitching events could suffice.

Hi Shawn,

I've enjoyed the inspirational and tactial-level information you and your guests share on *How to Be an Entrepreneur*.

I'm reaching out to see if you're looking for additional guests. I often speak about the need for entrepreneurs to train their mindset, in addition to mastering their craft. Is this something you'd be interested in chatting with? You can book a time here, but don't hesitate to reach out with additional questions via email as well.

Best,

Terry

terryrice.co

This is also a great opportunity for you to reference recent events their audience may be following and mention the fact you've been talking about it on social.

In any case, if you don't hear back, consider engaging with the host on social media. This is especially useful if you notice they didn't answer your previous email.

Email Marketing

Over time, your email list will grow through the events you attend and your lead magnet. However, you'll notice not everyone responded to your offer to follow up with a discovery call or reached out to you for more information. It's time for you to proactively reach out. You can do this via personalized emails as well as your periodic newsletter.

This involves sorting and ongoing maintenance of your list. Your personalized emails most likely have the highest chance of converting, so you wouldn't want to send them a mass email at the same time. Instead, incubate them during the prospecting phase, and only move them to your larger email list if it seems like a deal won't be closed in the near future.

Personalized Emails

These emails go out to people you have identified as having a high value for one reason or another. Perhaps it's a large opportunity, or you'd love to work with them so you can connect with their network. Maybe you just think they're an amazing person. Either way, you want to send them a bespoke message based on your understanding of who they are and their goals.

If you've already interacted with them, whether it be online or in person, they should be easy to identify. If they got on your list through a lead magnet or an event you led, you'll have to do some digging. This involves viewing your list in a spreadsheet, such as Excel or Google Sheets. Set up a filter to hide anyone with a Gmail, Yahoo, or any other extension that doesn't represent a unique website. I'm not saying high-value prospects don't use Gmail, but being able to identify the company a prospects works for by their email domain is a fast way to qualify them.

A client of mine leads workshops for startups in New York. One time, he forwarded me an email from an individual who didn't appear to fit his target audience based on the information provided in the intake form. He asked me what he could do to stop attracting these opportunities, or at least send them a templated response. I looked up the domain associated with her email address and eventually discovered she was responsible for scheduling 150 corporate workshops per year. We very quickly came up with a bespoke message to send her. A few months later, he landed an amazing opportunity that he almost didn't pursue. You should follow this same process with every person on your email list. If they seem like a great opportunity, send them a personalized email.

Next, you'll start looking up the names of people who don't have a corporate domain. The easiest way to find out more about them is via LinkedIn. However, depending on their subscription, they may be able to see you looked at their profile. That's not inherently bad, but it's also obvious you're researching them. If this happens, and they may be a good potential client, consider sending them a connection request. Since they should have some idea who you are, you can be a bit more formal, like this:

> Hey Noah,
>
> I'm leading a free workshop on best practices for landing podcast interviews and thought you might be interested. You can register via the link below. Let me know if you can make it, and don't hesitate to reach out with any questions.

This is a pretty simple approach. Notice how having an ongoing series of webinars comes in handy?

Other options include searching while you're in Incognito Mode or changing your LinkedIn setting to define what information people can see when you look at their profile. If you want to streamline this approach all together, I suggest having a virtual assistant perform this initial research.

The Outreach

Now that you've identified these high-value prospects, it's time to connect. You can follow the same approaches we covered in Chapter 8:

- ► Give a genuine compliment.
- ► Ask a genuine question.
- ► Lead with value.

Here's an example of how you can ask a genuine question:

Subject: Quick question about podcast appearances

Body:

> Hi Noah,
>
> Quick question for you. I noticed you've been posting a lot of value-driven content on LinkedIn lately. Your post about how to avoid burnout was particularly useful to me. I'm wondering, have you ever considered sharing your experience and point of view on podcasts?
>
> Look forward to hearing from you.

Best,

Terry Rice
Business Development Consultant
Would you like to chat? Book a time with me here.

This approach requires some research on your end, but it's also more likely to get a response. Once they respond, you can mention that upcoming webinar you have on landing podcast interviews, provided that's a good fit. Even if they aren't interested in appearing on podcasts, you can start the one-on-one communication process. You can then follow up by asking how their business is going with a goal of setting up an enrollment call. Just saying, "What would need to happen in order for you to consider this next year a success?" in your email can start that process.

You'll also notice I overtly mentioned the opportunity to book a call with me in my signature. I don't have this option available in my standard signature, but it's always visible for high-value prospects.

Of course, you can also get straight to the point and try to book an enrollment call.

Subject: Quick question about growing your business

Body:

Hi Noah,

Quick question for you. I noticed you've been posting a lot of value-driven content on LinkedIn lately. Your post about how to avoid burnout was particularly useful to me. I'm wondering, have you ever considered sharing your experience and point of view on podcasts? I'm leading a free workshop on best practices for landing podcast interviews and thought you might be interested.

If you can't make it, I'd still love to get a better understanding of how things are going with your business. Specifically, what would need to happen in order for you to consider this next year a success? Feel free to follow up via email or book a time with me below.

Look forward to hearing from you!

Best,

Terry Rice
Business Development Consultant
Would you like to chat? Book a time with me here.

Notice there were two direct asks in the email. You don't want to include more than that since it can be confusing. In this case, my second question provided an open alternative if Noah had no interest in attending the podcast.

Personalized emails take time, but they'll go a long way in regard to making a more genuine connection. You've chosen to reach out to these individuals for a reason; now give them a reason to respond.

Your Newsletter

Nurturing your email list involves sending out content that provides value to your subscribers. The goal is to keep them engaged, stay on their radar, and prime them to potentially work with you in the future. This is particularly beneficial if you eventually release a product with a relatively low price point, such as a $300 online course. On average, about 1 percent of people on your list will convert into buyers.

If you decided to have an ongoing newsletter, you don't want it to feel like a part-time job. You may discover the majority of clients you book do so within a few months of meeting you, before you even moved them to the newsletter phase. Again, this is why it's so important to track the source of your converting leads. Way too many consultants spend hours formatting their newsletter or scrambling to find something to say, not realizing they're reaching out to an audience that has a low potential to convert. That time may have been better spent sending personalized emails to high-value prospects or posting really great content on LinkedIn.

To streamline the process, it's beneficial to have a template you almost always follow. If you haven't already, join the email list of competitors or people who serve the same audience as you. This will give you an idea of how they communicate, and you may pick up some tips you can leverage. Part of being a consultant involves building a personal brand. Therefore, you should tell personal stories in your emails, then let the audience know how it applies to them. Here's an example from my own newsletter:

Subject: The benefits of having a clearly defined sales approach

Body:

Hi there,

You can't be the best version of yourself if you don't prioritize your health. Although this is often a trend in the new year, you'll want to make this part of your lifestyle. Fortunately, my gym is in the building next door to my coworking space so it's relatively easy for me to work out during the day. I can leave the gym at 10:55 and be at my desk by 11:00.

This past week as I was casually strolling out of the gym, I looked down and noticed I had a call with a prospect that started in four minutes! That's barely enough time to make a protein shake, let alone prep for a call. As I'm sure you know, you could have the best solution out there, but you could easily tank a deal if you don't present yourself in the right light. Confidence, combined with a road map aligned with success, is what ultimately wins the day.

Although I was in a rush, I still made a protein shake, no need to show up late and hangry. With about a minute to spare, I made myself look somewhat presentable and kicked off the call.

It went extremely well. Why? Because even though I was running late, I was still prepared. As I've shared before my personal philosophy is to be purpose-driven, prepared, and patient. Being prepared with a defined approach to the call allowed me to easily structure the conversation, even though I had to wipe beads of sweat off my forehead every few minutes! I have a list of five questions that I ask during every call. Now, this might sound counterintuitive. Isn't every person and opportunity unique? Absolutely! That's the benefit of having a defined process. Once you determine what needs to take place, you can be as creative or bespoke as you would like. Imagine you're watching a dance competition where everyone has to do the tango. There are certain steps and movements that are clearly understood to be the tango; that's the process. However, as long as you meet that criteria, you can be as expressive as you'd like.

On enrollment calls, you don't want to sound like a robot, but you do need to follow an established process. This gives you the freedom to deploy emotional intelligence and empathy, while still gathering the information you need.

I documented these questions in my latest article, "5 Questions Every Consultant Must Ask During a Sales Call," which you can view on my website. One of my favorites is "What would need to happen in order for you to feel good about your results?" That question will tell you specifically what you need to deliver on in order to win their business and make them happy.

If you have any questions, consider joining my upcoming webinar where I'll go deeper into these questions and answer any questions you may have. You can sign up here. All registered attendees will get a copy of the recording.

Looking for more 1:1 input? Book a discovery call with me here. You'll have to excuse me if I look like I just got back from the gym. Got to prioritize your health!

Looking forward,

Terry

Notice how I started off by saying "Hi there"? Sure many programs allow you to put the person's first name in your email, but you may not have that for one reason or another. If you don't just go with "Hi there" or "Hello," don't make it any more formal than that.

As I mentioned earlier, my goal was to tell a story that would provide value to my audience. I only asked for something at the very end—the prompt for an enrollment call. Be sure not to be overly salesy with these emails. Just because they're on your list doesn't mean they won't unsubscribe! Focus on providing value with 80 percent of the content, and promoting yourself with the remaining 20 percent.

Know When to Send, and How Often

According to Mailchimp, Tuesday, Wednesday, and Thursday have traditionally been favorite days to send email campaigns. Many people are dragging on Monday, then kicking and screaming on Friday. MailChimp confirms that Tuesday and Thursday are the two most popular days to send email newsletters.

What is the best time to send your emails? It depends. Historically, the best time was 8 A.M. to 10 A.M. Unfortunately, anyone who Googles "best time to send an email" will get the same result, which could increase your competition. It also depends on your audience. A somewhat younger or tech savvy audience is more likely to open their emails on a mobile device. That being said, there's no use driving yourself crazy about the best time to send until you start getting some real data in. Most platforms will give you reporting on when your email was opened, allowing you to optimize as you see fit. MailChimp also offers Send Time Optimization, which uses data science to determine when your contacts are most likely to engage, and sends your emails at that time.

How often should you send? That depends as well. How often can you come up with something interesting to say? Or what results are you getting from your emails? If you're emailing once per week and getting very little results, you'll either need to adjust your copy strategy or perhaps focus on other marketing activities.

I suggest starting off by emailing once per month. This should give you enough time to create great content, while still performing other activities to grow and manage your business. If you notice you're getting amazing results (measured by opens, replies, clicks, and conversions), consider increasing the frequency. However, make sure this doesn't cause a spike in unsubscribes or a decrease in engagement. To make things easier consider repurposing a blog you recently wrote, similar to what I did in the previous example.

Always include a call to action! You don't have to be overly salesy, but you need to remind them you're in business.

Cold Calling

Within a few months of launching my business, I purposely did something to step out of my comfort zone. I walked into an apparel shop in Brooklyn and pitched myself as a Facebook marketing expert. I clumsily described my services, and they said yes. I couldn't believe it actually worked. I also never did it again.

Jake Savage is an expert at cold calling, both in-person and via phone. In a previous job, he knocked on just under 100,000 doors selling home remodeling products. When knee injury sidelined him for three months, he focused on cold calling over the phone.

Cold calling does work, but you have to have the right mindset for it. I don't. Fortunately, Jake Savage does. Take a look at some more of his tips:

- *Disrupt their expectations.* People rarely answer calls from unknown numbers, and if they do, they're likely expecting a robot call. Be authentic (human) as quickly as you can. "Hey, is this Bill?" Acknowledge that the call is out of the blue before you mention your name or what you do then acknowledge something relevant to them.
- *Don't act like everything is completely normal.* It's not. Justify why you chose to call them versus emailing/messaging them. "Hey, Bill. I know this is completely out of the blue but I thought I'd try you on the phone since I saw your company recently got into Whole Foods nationwide!"
- *Introduce yourself and use artificial time constraints.* Studies show that awkwardness in a conversation does not stem from the person or the topic. It stems from not being sure where the conversation is headed. Relieve this tension/awkwardness by stating a specific time frame. "My name's Jake Savage and I'm one of the co-owners here at Basemakers. I'm sure you're in the middle of something, and I actually have to run in about five minutes so I'll make it quick."
- *State your reason for calling.* "I figured you probably get a ton of emails every day, so I thought I'd give you a ring. We're a merchandising and sales support team for a lot of companies just like yours inside of Whole Foods."
- *Convey you're not desperate.* "And actually, I'm not even sure this could be a good fit. I just figured I'd call and introduce myself."
- *Set up the next conversation.* "I don't know if you've given much thought yet to in-store support, but do you think you'd be open to connecting about it more another time?" There you have it. One more thing I would suggest is don't talk too fast. You may be in a hurry to get through what you have to say or get a response from the prospect, but you still want to make sure they understand what you're saying.

Snail Mail

Although snail mail is a traditional form of advertising, a study showed millennials are open to it. The study found 38 percent of millennials stated they like receiving newsletters/mail from orgs not seeking donations compared to 28 percent who say they dislike it. I should note, this study was conducted by the United States Postal Service, so we can assume there's an opportunity for bias.

However, it's still worth considering. My friend Janine Labriola owns a gym in Brooklyn, Park Fitness BK (www.parkfitnessbk.com), which holds several scheduled fitness classes throughout the day. She tried her hand at Facebook ads but just wasn't able to make it work. As a local gym, she needed a way to easily reach people who lived in the apartments located near her gym. She eventually used snail mail to promote her free trial classes. For less than $500 she was able to print and mail postcards to all the units in several buildings within walking distance of her gym. To redeem the free class, people had to bring in the postcard she sent; this allowed her to track the response rate. Janine was so pleased with the results she repeated the same process every quarter.

If you find yourself in a similar situation, this could be a route worth exploring. For example, the woman who helped us select a school for our daughter could send flyers to areas in Brooklyn that young families tend to live in. For consultants who offer services to a broader audience, such as financial services, you can cast an even wider net.

Sending mail is relatively cheap, though designing and printing something presentable comes at a cost. As with any tactic, you'll need to make sure you're tracking results so you can determine what you're getting for your money and effort.

Why This Is Important

Although you can win business by doing in-person events and word-of-mouth adverting from your network, you need to develop a more robust business development strategy. For many consultants, this became even more apparent during the COVID shutdown when the ability to network and deliver content in person was put on hold.

You'll eventually discover what approaches work best for you based on your personality, audience, and innate capabilities. The key is to get started so you home in on your preferred tactics and always provide value in exchange for your audience's attention.

Action Items

▶ Consider creating video content. You can start with the ten questions and responses previously developed.

▶ Determine webinar topics that would provide value to your audience, and promote them via social and email.

▶ Research and connect with podcasts that your target audience listens to, and track results in your CRM.

▶ Determine the structure and content of your outbound email marketing, and research by subscribing to the email lists of other independent consultants.

▶ Complete the Finding & Attracting Clients section of The One Page Business Plan.

Pitching and Proposals

You've come up with an amazing offer, provided value to your audience, and now people are reaching out saying, "How can you help me?" It's time to get on the phone or connect in person and have an enrollment call. You might feel excited or a little nervous, and that's perfectly natural. You know the value you can provide. This call is simply your opportunity to learn more about the prospect's challenges and discuss how you may be able to assist.

Mike Swigunski sets himself up for success by making sure he's chatting with the right people in the first place. "I really qualify my leads before hopping on any call, then I follow my fine-tuned slide deck and have a 50 percent close rate." He adds: "Focus on the outcome; sell the end product and not features." Mike makes an excellent point. When the time comes to speak about how you can help, be sure to highlight the transformation your client is seeking.

Of course, you can't understand the transformation they seek without asking the right questions. Natalie Allport provides additional guidance here:

> *I try to listen more than I speak. Asking more questions, such as business goals, personal goals of the business owner, current challenges, and other such questions will help qualify the lead in the first place, as well as get the required amount of information you need to give advice or suggest services/solutions.*

Kellen Driscoll reiterates the value of asking questions. "I have a dedicated process when I have a sales call. I have an entire breakdown and script that I follow and make my own. The questions I ask are centered around the following: goals, solutions, action items, and getting to the root of the real problem." Questions such as, "Other than price, is there anything that would keep you from doing business with me today?" allow you to isolate objections and address them accordingly.

Like Kellen and every other expert mentioned, you'll eventually develop your own process and find a way to make it your own.

Tina has a meeting with Spencer coming up in just a few days. This could be her first closed deal so she's understandably nervous. She knows the best way to overcome this is to be prepared. That same approach applies to you as well. In this chapter, we'll discuss how you can confidently present the value of your services and quickly send over proposals with a pain-free and predictable process.

Pitching

If you don't have a "salesy" personality, pitching your services can be terrifying. Fortunately, you don't need to be salesy. You just need to have a genuine desire to help

tip

A deep dive into emotional intelligence is outside the scope of this book, but I highly recommend reading up on the topic. *Entrepreneur Voices on Emotional Intelligence* presents you with real-world strategies that can be extremely helpful.

your clients and be able to deploy a sufficient level of emotional intelligence. You already have the former, and the latter can be developed over time.

For now, just remember this pitch isn't about you or your background. It's about the client and developing a deeper understanding of their needs. You should be listening more than you talk, but you'll need to make sure you're receiving the right information. Beyond that, this isn't even a pitch in the traditional sense—it's an enrollment conversation. After you understand the prospect's needs, you'll explain how you can create a course of action to get them where they want to be. At the end they'll either enroll, or they won't. You want them to be excited about the potential of partnering with you. You never want to feel like you talked them into doing something they didn't fully understand or aren't completely committed to.

The pitch is all about dialogue. Let's use our fictional friends Tina and Spencer to show all the nuances of the five questions you must ask during any enrollment conversation.

Question 1: What's Going On, and How Is It Affecting Your Life?

You most likely have some information about your potential client before entering this conversation. You can use that to tee things up, but you'll still want them to essentially start from scratch. The more information you can get about their specific needs, the better you'll be able to explain how you can help them, assuming you can. If you can't help them, this is the time to make that known so you both can move on. Maybe you have a colleague who can help, or you have some resources that might help. That said, be honest about what you can and cannot do for the potential client. The "fake it till you make it" approach is a good way to damage your reputation, and it's not right to waste someone's time and money. Hopefully, you're still in a position to help them, and you can continue asking probing questions.

If you're able to quantify revenue impact—how much money they have to gain or lose based on their current challenge or opportunity—this will make it easier for you to explain your fees later on. Reason being, you'll be able to show them a clear ROI from the partnership. However, some challenges aren't associated with revenue, such as the inability to get a sufficient night's sleep. In this case, you'll want to better understand how this problem is affecting their personal life.

Take notes, and ask them to pause if necessary. It's not rude; you're proving that you have a genuine need to understand their challenge. Here's what that conversation might look like:

Tina: I'm glad we were able to set up a time to chat. I understand you want to implement a CRM system, but can you give me more background on the situation?

Spencer: We need to get organized, and we're not sure where to start. Can you explain how you normally help people in my position?

The prospective client may immediately ask you to explain what you do and how you can help them. Don't do that! This part of the conversation is all about them, not you. Here is one way to handle that question, using our avatar, Tina, as the example:

Tina: I help small businesses increase their revenue and retention by implementing customer relationship management systems. Since many small business owners wear many hats, I do my best to make this as simple as possible. Can you give me an idea of how you're currently managing leads and following up with customer inquiries?

This pivot is important. Tina answered the question, which was basically her positioning statement with added context, she then shifted the conversation back to Spencer.

Spencer: It's actually a bit of a mess. I have spreadsheets and random notes tracking all these leads. I'm usually trying to write so quickly I can barely read anything. Afterward, I'll notice I forgot to ask them some critical questions. The customer service piece isn't organized either. Sometimes it takes us weeks to get a response out just because we assumed someone else already took care of it. We often don't realize it until we see a negative comment on social media.

Tina: OK, so it sounds like you're not converting as many leads as you'd like to, which obviously has a negative impact on revenue. Can you give me information on your current conversion rate and average order value?

Spencer: Sure, we're currently converting about 10 percent of leads, from what I can tell. I'm sure we could get that up to 20 percent if we were actually keeping track of them in a more systematic way. Prospects end up chasing us instead of the other way around. Some of them don't bother chasing at all and just go with another vendor. Our average order value is about $5,000, and we do around 20 deals per quarter.

Heads up, this part is about to get into some quick but detailed math. You'll need to learn how to do this, too. It's totally fine to whip out a calculator during these chats, if necessary. The more specific your understanding of their problem, rooted in real numbers, the better you'll be able to quantify the revenue impact.

Tina: Got it. So at around $5,000 per order and 20 deals per quarter, that's $100,000 in revenue per quarter. If you're converting 10 percent of deals, that means you had 200 leads. You feel like you could easily close 20 percent if you managed these leads better, but let's just be conservative and say you increase your close rate to 15 percent. If you have 200 leads, and close 15 percent of them, that comes out to 30 closed deals. With an average order value of $5,000, you would make $150,000 in revenue per quarter instead of $100,000. Does that sound right to you?

Spencer: Yes, conservatively. We can bring in even more during Q2 when sports teams are gearing up for the summer.

Tina: So you're already up $50,000, not to mention the revenue impact of poor customer service. That part is a bit more challenging to calculate, but I'm sure your lifetime value will increase if you keep more of your customers happy. You also won't have to worry about losing deals due to negative reviews and comments on social media.

Spencer: You're right. That part is hard to quantify, but I know it's hurting us. It's not just about revenue; we want to make our customers happy. Things just seem to fall through the cracks all the time.

Tina managed to quantify the revenue impact and how it impacts Spencer's personal life. She can now move on to the next question.

Question 2: What Have You Already Tried to Address This Problem?

The prospective client's response to this question will help you in a couple of ways.:

▶ You won't recommend solutions that have failed for a legitimate reason.
▶ You'll be able to course-correct solutions that could have been successful with the proper guidance.

Beyond that, you'll also get better insight into how important solving for this challenge is and the pain associated with this resolution. This is also your time to show genuine empathy by paraphrasing and hypothesizing. Here is an example of how this part of the conversation might happen between Tina and Spencer:

Tina: OK, glad we're aligned here. So, how have you already tried to address this problem?

Spencer: We tried keeping track of everything on an Excel sheet. People were supposed to update the sheet, then email an updated copy. That rarely happened so we were constantly working off the wrong version. Then, we tried using Google

Sheets, but some people just didn't get how to use it. There was an intern who was good at training people, but she left without documenting anything.

Tina: So what I'm hearing is, the systems you previously implemented either weren't a good fit, or you didn't get the proper onboarding. I can see how this would be frustrating. Sometimes people prefer to stick with a system they understand, even if it's slower.

Spencer: Exactly. We didn't empower them to embrace all these changes we came up with. It caused a bit of anxiety too. People were concerned they were going to lose their jobs if they didn't learn the new system.

Tina: Sounds like proper onboarding, documentation, and continued support are necessary to get the results we're looking for.

Just like that, Tina picked up on a few levers she can use to create an irresistible offer for Spencer. Having a great solution isn't enough. She'll need to reference long-term support. Fortunately, she can add this to her fee.

Question 3: What Are Some Approaches or Resources You Haven't Explored?

This can easily be one of the most unselfish questions you ask a prospective client. They may determine there's another internal resource or someone they could hire full-time to solve this challenge. You may be able to assist or reengage if the problem persists after they attempt to solve it on their own. Let's see how Tina handles this question:

Tina: OK, so what are some other approaches or resources you haven't explored yet?

Spencer: To be honest, at this point I'm done exploring. I need to focus on running my entire business. I'd love for someone to come in and just help me get this part straight.

This response is common. Often, prospects want you to be the filter for other approaches or resources. Even if they hire someone in-house, they may want you to find or vet this individual.

Question 4: What Would Need to Happen for You to Feel Good About Our Results?

Get ready to take notes on the prospect's response. They'll tell you exactly what they want from you and exactly what would earn you a referral or testimonial. Quantify or qualify as much as possible. After they respond, you can start talking more about how you can help. If you can't help, be honest with them and yourself.

Tina: Based on all this, what would need to happen in order for you to feel good about our results? What outcomes are you looking for?

Spencer: Well, we already talked about increasing our conversion rate, which would be amazing. What I really want is to be able to see where I'm getting leads from, connect with these leads properly, and determine how to find more clients that convert. I just want to reduce the uncertainty in regard to how much revenue we'll bring in from month to month. It's hard to plan for anything, including vacations with my family, when I have no clue how much money we'll bring in this year. I always feel like I should be doing something instead of relaxing. My kids are starting to get older, and they pick up on this, too.

Tina: I can definitely relate; I'm also a business owner, and I know how frustrating that lack of clarity can be. That's why I enjoy helping people like you streamline their business process by implementing a CRM system. Like you said though, just setting up a system isn't enough if your team doesn't feel comfortable. In addition to implementation, I provide live training and document every process covered. We cover a lot during the training, but I'm also available to field any questions that come up after. Sometimes people feel like they've nailed it during training, but it's easy to get confused when you do something for the first time solo.

Spencer: Yep, you nailed it. I know it will take people time to get used to it, but we'll also save a lot of time and make more money going forward.

Tina: You'll finally be able to go on vacation, too, right?

Spencer: Exactly. My kids would enjoy that a lot.

Spencer reinforced his goals but also talked about his vision. Tina can then speak to both of them in her response. Notice she did talk about herself, but it was only in context to Spencer's situation. If a prospect wants to know more about you, they'll ask. Be prepared to answer exactly how you help clients. This is where your defined service comes in.

Question 5: *Would You Like My Help?*

Always ask during the call, overtly, if the prospect wants your help. This can lead to a no, yes, or more probing questions. Don't say, "Well, I can send you some more information . . ." or "Would you like to think about it and set up another time to call?" Just ask. If they want more information or to think about it, they'll tell you. Of course, you should ask this question only if you actually want to work with the client. Even if you're selling your services, you should always be the buyer. A bad client is toxic to your business and mindset. I've never regretted saying no to a prospect, but I have regretted saying yes, especially when something in my gut told me it was a bad idea. Let's see how Tina makes the ask:

> *Tina*: I'm clear on what's going on, and I feel we could solve for these challenges together. Would you like my help?

> *Spencer*: I need to noodle this over for a day or so, but I'm feeling good about it. I'm relieved to know there's a clear path forward. We've been struggling with this forever. Can you send over a proposal?

> *Tina*: Absolutely. I'm just going to send over a document summarizing everything first. Once we're clear on that, I can send a proposal. Would that work for you?

> *Spencer*: Sure thing. I'll take a look at it as soon as it hits my inbox.

> *Tina*: Great. Also, what are you looking for in the proposal? Any specific details?

> *Spencer*: Nothing too complicated, but please explain the ongoing training services. That part is very important.

The summary document is optional. In some cases, you can go ahead and send a proposal. However, if this a more bespoke project, you'll have to think about your approach and see if that aligns with the client's expectations.

Proposals

My proposals used to take forever to write. I'd go back and forth trying to make everything perfect and copying "official sounding" language that I found online. Unfortunately, the longer it takes you to send out a proposal, the less likely it is to get approved. People may lose interest, or find another solution, or the budget can get used elsewhere.

Over time, I discovered writing proposals doesn't have to be that challenging. You just have to prepare yourself properly:

▶ Take notes, and check for understanding. Before even sending a proposal, summarize the prospect's needs, then check with them to make sure you have everything correct. Ask if there is anything they would add or take away from the scope you've outlined. You'll want to do this via email for greater accuracy.

▶ Ask the prospect what they expect to see in a proposal and who needs to see it. They may want something extremely simple that can be churned out in a few minutes. Or the decision may have to go through several people who were not present during your previous conversations. In this case, more details may be necessary.

▶ Develop a template that can be easily customized. There's no need to reinvent the wheel every time. Basic content such as your name, location, and terms of service aren't going to change.

▶ Make it easy for them to sign. Don't send a PDF that requires them to print, sign, scan, and email. Use an electronic signature program, such as DocuSign.

Although you want to be well prepared, don't feel pressured to make it perfect. If the prospect genuinely wants to work with you, they'll follow up with any necessary edits. I once sent a client a proposal that still included some of the information from another proposal I found online. It was extremely obvious since it made no sense whatsoever. They noticed the weirdness and simply asked me to correct it. You may also have to revise a proposal due to an unforeseeable internal requirement. This back and forth can be nerve wracking, but you're still moving forward.

I strongly suggest tracking opens and clicks on the email your proposal was included in. This can easily be accomplished through the reporting feature in via HubSpot and various other email programs. This is beneficial for a few reasons:

▶ You won't drive yourself crazy wondering if the prospect received it or not. You'll know exactly when they opened it and how. If a prospect opens your proposal on their cell phone and doesn't immediately get back to you, they may be putting it off until they're in front of a computer.

▶ You'll have a better understanding of when you should follow up. If five days go by with no response, but you notice they opened it on the sixth day, you'll want to follow up the next day.

Determining when to follow up can also be a challenge. You don't want to seem too salesy or desperate. On the other hand, the phrase "fortune is in the follow-up" rings true. You need to assess each opportunity separately. If the prospect says they need to think about it a certain amount of time, respect their boundaries. I typically wait a week to follow up after sending a proposal. Instead of saying something basic like, "Just checking to see if you had a chance to review my proposal," I go with the following approach:

I noticed (something relevant about them, their company, or industry), which prompted me to see if you'd like to schedule another chat over the next week or so, but I completely understand if you need more time to digest.

Again, I'd be excited to work with you and I'm available to answer any questions you may have. Feel free to shoot me an email or schedule another call with me here.

Also, I found a great article that speaks to the exact challenge you referenced around onboarding new business processes. I hope you find it helpful.

If you still don't hear back after another week, things aren't looking great. Of course, you'll want to follow up one more time, but you'll need to manage your expectations. Here is what you can say in your second follow-up:

Reaching out again to see if you're still interested in partnering together. Based on our conversation, I believe I can help you in the following ways:

▶ *Relevant value offering*

▶ *Relevant value offering*

▶ *Relevant value offering*

That said, I know this is a big decision, so I understand if you need to think about it longer. Don't hesitate to reach out with any questions or schedule another call with me here.

This is where I would stop pitching, but there's no harm in following up with additional information that may be valuable to the prospect. For example, you could send another relevant article or industry benchmark report. Start a new email thread so you don't come off as passive aggressive. Remember, you are focusing on long-term relationships, not just making a quick buck.

Next Steps

It can be hard not to take it personally when proposals don't get approved, especially if you were almost positive they would. You can drive yourself crazy wondering what went wrong. While I fully support reflecting and looking for opportunities to improve, you may not have done anything wrong. The prospect could have simply lost interest, not been able to secure the budget, or just went with another provider. In a utopian situation, you'd get a direct answer as to why you didn't win the business. If not, just keep it moving so you can be ready for the next opportunity.

Hopefully, you won their business and can move on to delivering on your promises.

Why This Is Important

As we've said before, clarity is the precursor to confidence. The clearer you are on your overall pitching and proposal process, the more confident you'll become. But even when you prepare in advance, be sure to stay present in the conversation so you can glean more insights. Asking probing questions may help you get a better understanding of the situation and prove you're looking at things from their perspective.

Although it's great to win deals, remember the enrollment call is also meant for you to filter out people you may not want to work with for one reason or another. Even as the seller, you should always be the buyer.

Action Items

▶ Practice the five enrollment call questions.. Based on your empathy map, hypothesize how your audience would respond.

▶ Determine if you need to add or remove any questions. What else would help you better understand your audience's challenges and how you can help?

▶ Ask a friend or colleague to play the role of prospect so you can practice in real time.

▶ Draft proposal templates that can be augmented for specific use cases.

▶ Document your follow-up email sequence, and save these as templates.

Your First Clients and Commitment to Excellence

Now that your client has signed the contract, it's time to start providing value. But beware—this is where imposter syndrome can start to sink in. You may feel like you're not worthy of the amount you charged, or you're concerned you're going to mess something up. This feeling is natural, and the best way to combat it is to deliver on the promises you made.

Still, you're bound to hit a few bumps in the road along the way. The best approach is to learn from your mistakes without letting them have a negative impact on your progress or self-worth. Like any entrepreneur, you'll need to get accustomed to pivoting.

Meg McKeen shares an example from her experience:

My first offering was a bust; simply stated, I overbuilt it. I recognized this quickly and stripped the program down to its most essential and salable components and began offering those à la carte. From there, cues from my clients told me what they needed, and as it made sense for me and how I wanted my time and energy to be spent in my work, I developed additional offerings. So it's important to remember that your first idea doesn't have to be your last, and tweaking is a natural part of the getting-started process.

Mike Swigunski can speak to this as well. Shortly after launching his training program, he cut the length in half. "Focus on the results and pick the fastest realistic way to get there. I assumed an eight-week sprint would work best, but eventually realized four worked best for my students and sales cycle."

And, although you may be in a rush to rapidly grow your business, Natalie Allport cautions you to take it slow and steady. "Focus on relationships more than quick sales. Some operations of business can be replaced by automation, but relationships can't. Make sure you build a great relationship with that first client before you seek others."

Your first client took a chance on you. This chapter walks through how to reward them with exceptional service, develop a repeatable customer service model, and ask for your first referral. You'll also discover where to draw the line when it comes to the extent of time dedicated to one project.

Onboarding

Your goal is to be the best business partner any of your clients work with. That all starts with the onboarding process.

You'll want to start by giving them access to a cloud-based platform you'll both be using for organization and storage. This could be a project management system, such as Asana. You could also use a shared Google Drive folder. Either way, you don't want to store things locally or in an email thread. Keep in mind, training them how to use these tools is part of the onboarding process.

I start each engagement with a detailed questionnaire. This goes much deeper than the questions asked during the enrollment conversation and is delivered via Google Doc. If you use a Google Drive folder, you can just keep creating a new copy of all your documents every time you need to onboard a new client.

This folder I share with clients includes several documents, including the following:

▶ How to create a personal brand statement
▶ How to define your service offering
▶ Email templates for pitching speaking opportunities
▶ Messaging templates for prospecting on LinkedIn
▶ Tracking action items and results

The amount of content you have preprepared will evolve over time, but you need to start with a solid plan for how you'll onboard clients. Again, this will help alleviate impostor syndrome.

If you plan on having regularly scheduled calls or in-person meetings, now is a good time to start scheduling them. This way, you'll always be prepared and won't have to worry about rushing from one appointment to another. I make sure my clients have first choice in regard to booking time on my calendar. Blocking this time off in advance helps me avoid someone else taking a time slot they may have wanted. Telling a client your schedule is booked with the exception of 4:30 on Friday usually doesn't go over very well.

Developing a Road Map

As an extension of the onboarding process, you'll need to develop a project road map. What are the action items you'll be tackling, and when? I use Google Sheets for this because it's easy for most clients to understand, and they can easily tag me if any questions come up. Platforms such as Asana and Trello can help with this as well.

It's important to keep this updated. If things get delayed for one reason or another, you'll also have to make adjustments. Keep an eye out for anything that would cause this engagement to take longer than originally planned. Make these concerns known as soon as possible, and don't wait for your client to bring it up. It may be an uncomfortable conversation, but they'll appreciate the fact you addressed it before they did.

Here is a quick look at a sample project road map in Figure 12–1 on page 156.

Tracking Progress

Sometimes it's challenging to see progress on a micro level. This is why it's important to track behaviors and actions that are aligned with making progress.

One of the services I provide is helping my clients land paid speaking gigs, which involves them reaching out to organizations that host these opportunities.

FIGURE 12–1: **Project Road Map**

To track progress, we do the following in Google Sheets:

▶ Make a list of organizations to contact.

▶ Track when an initial email was sent.

▶ Record any responses.

On my end, I'm able to see they're executing on the plan we've outlined. If they haven't, I can step in and provide guidance or accountability. As responses start coming in, they get to see the results of their effort. Keep in mind, it can take months before they get a solid confirmation.

Of course, you may have totally different actions to track. Maybe it's the number of days they meditated last week, or how many processes they documented for a new CRM system. Either way, this documentation allows you to easily illustrate how much you've accomplished over any given period of time.

Seek Ongoing Feedback

If you previously worked for a company, you most likely had check-ins or more formal reviews with your manager to chart your performance. Many employees dread these for one reason or another. As an independent consultant, you're going to voluntarily put yourself in this situation. Seek feedback constantly, not after several weeks or after a project has ended.

Keep in mind that not every client will tell you when something is wrong. They'll just never work with you again, and they definitely won't recommend you. They also may not realize it's OK to feel like things are a bit "off." Ask probing questions to gauge where they're at in terms of how they feel about working with you. Here's the most impactful question you can ask: "Based on our progress, do you still feel good about the decision to work with me?"

Now, keep in mind, you may not have been able to deliver obvious results at this time. But they should be able to give input on your onboarding and communication. Here's how this could look with Tina and Spencer:

> *Tina*: I'd like to check in and see how things are going so far. Based on our progress, do you still feel good about the decision to work with me?

> *Spencer*: Yes, I do. I'm just confused about a lot of the processes, but I guess it just takes some getting used to.

> *Tina*: Thanks for letting me know. What part confuses you?

> *Spencer*: Well, I'm documenting all these processes so we can include them in our CRM, but it takes forever. I feel like it takes me three times longer because I have to be so detailed in my descriptions. To be honest, I've just decided I'll do a few things manually instead of adding it to the list we're developing.

> *Tina*: It's perfectly normal to feel that way. I know it can be quicker just to do things yourself. The benefit of detailed documentation is not having to do it again going forward. It might take you 30 minutes this week, but it will save you 30 hours over the next year. Would it help if I taught you how to record your documentation instead of writing it? I can have the recordings transcribed after.

> *Spencer*: Yes, that would be great! I just can't type that fast so it's a bit of a pain. Recording the process would be much easier.

Unforeseen situations like this come up all the time, but they often aren't discussed unless you bring it up. In this example, Tina was able to solve Spencer's challenge and develop a new process she can use with other clients going forward.

You can also solicit more formal feedback. Examples include sending clients a survey created in Google Forms or routinely asking for a JOT (just one thing) you could improve.

Setting Boundaries

I once signed a client on a Friday afternoon. He needed help with his Facebook marketing campaigns, which I was happy to do. The next day he emailed me complaining about the lack of progress I made. I had to read the email twice to make sure I wasn't misunderstanding him. He told me he was under a lot of pressure to fix his campaigns, so he was going to put that pressure on me. I emailed him back, on Monday, and let him know I don't work over the weekends. I also flagged his comment about intentionally putting pressure on me, which I took as annoying at best. He apologized, but within a few days the behavior continued and I had to part ways with him.

Like many consultants, I started my company so I could have more control over my own schedule and the environment I worked in. You should do the same. Be very clear about your personal boundaries. Ask yourself:

- ▶ Do you want to take calls after traditional working hours?
- ▶ Is it OK for a client to add you to a Slack channel? (You'll definitely get interrupted more often.)
- ▶ Can a client text you, or do you prefer email?

You'll also want to keep an eye out for *scope creep*, which is when clients intentionally or unintentionally expand the scope of a project. Be prepared to push back on this and refer to the original contract and road map you both agreed on. Of course, you'll want to do this politely.

The bottom line is, you need to be compensated for the additional work that clients add to your plate.

Once you discuss the revised scope of work, the client may be willing to pay you for expanding the scope of the original deal.

Before you even offer that as an option, though, you'll first want to consider a things:

- ▶ Is this something you're capable of and want to do?
- ▶ Do you need to bring in additional resources to complete this additional aspect of the project?
- ▶ Will committing impact another client or your desired lifestyle?
- ▶ Will this distract you from further developing your core competencies?

If you feel shaky about committing, trust your instincts.

Maintain a Commitment to Excellence

Referrals are one of the best ways to get new clients. Testimonials help people feel more comfortable with you. If you approach every opportunity thinking *"What do I need to do to get a referral or testimonial from this client?,"* you'll have no problem scaling your business. I'm not saying this should be your motivation. You should genuinely want to help people.

But, if you apply this thought process to the value you produce, you'll be able to make people happy and grow your business at the same time.

Positioning yourself as a business partner as opposed to service provider is a great way to go above and beyond what your clients expect.

- ▶ Did you see industry-related news they may find interesting or useful? Send it their way.
- ▶ Do you know of someone who could use their product or service? Pass along a referral.
- ▶ Is there another vendor or service that can help save time or money? Make them aware of it.
- ▶ I've been able to make clients happier just by pointing out a typo in their latest LinkedIn post. It's not necessarily a revenue-generating tip, but they like knowing I'm looking out for their best interest.

This commitment to excellence will earn you referrals and testimonials, but you'll typically still need to ask for them. Let's see how this would look between Tina and Spencer after their project has been completed:

Spencer: Thanks so much for the work you've done. I was able to go home early last Friday for the first time in ages. It took some getting used to, but I feel so much more confident in regard to how we're running our business. For years, we were accidentally successful. Now, we have a solid process and plan in place to scale that success.

Tina: That's so great to hear. I'm glad we were able to iron out all those wrinkles, and I appreciate the support from you and your team. One of the ways I grow my business is through referrals. Would you feel comfortable letting other people know about the results we've been able to accomplish? If possible, I'd love to have a quote from you on my website as well. What you just said would be perfect.

Spencer: Of course, I've already started talking to some of the other members about you. I'm happy to help.

The best time to ask for a referral or testimonial is immediately after you've received praise from a client. It's clear they enjoy working with you, and you can pretty much just ask them to repeat whatever they already said or wrote. You may feel shy about asking, but don't. If you've done a good job, many clients will be happy to help you out.

Even if they say no, you'll most likely gain valuable feedback in regard to why they would rather not refer you at that time. If they offered critical input on your performance, you could take this as a learning opportunity.

That said, some clients may not feel comfortable due to personal or professional reasons. Maybe you offer services they'd rather keep private, or they don't want their competitors to know about their competitive advantage. Respect their boundaries, and find other ways to boost your credibility, for example, a relevant media appearance or impactful blog post.

Why This Is Important

A solid onboarding experience sets the stage for a successful project and relationship. It will help alleviate impostor syndrome and reinforce why the client chose to work with you. Keep in mind, this will evolve over time. If you find yourself continually asking the same questions or requesting the same resources over and over again, add this to your onboarding process.

Your road map is pivotal to making sure you're keeping up with project milestones and being able to celebrate the small accomplishments that are part of a larger project.

Proactively asking for feedback will greatly aid in your professional development and increase client satisfaction. Of course, you may not be able to implement every piece of feedback they provide. Be sure to determine your personal and professional boundaries and to avoid distraction and burnout.

Action Items

- ▶ Develop your onboarding process, including any associated shared drives and templates.
- ▶ Create a road map template that can be augmented for specific uses cases.
- ▶ Determine and document your feedback process.
- ▶ Determine the personal and professional boundaries you'll establish.

Scaling Success and Managing Employees

For many businesses, scaling is part of the game plan, so long as you can do so efficiently. Managers are brought on to oversee the day-to-day activities of their team while providing guidance along the way. These managers are largely recognized for the impact of their overall team as opposed to their individual achievements. Additionally, the time it takes to manage this team is understood by all stakeholders.

Natalie Allport decided to take on employees after initially starting out solo. She recalls, "I learned a lot about how to manage employees, which is something I had not done or had before. That was a challenge in itself, especially for solopreneurs diving into having a team or another employee on board." Taking on employees adds another layer of complexity, but it can also be beneficial to be part of a team, and it's a great way to scale. You'll just need to make sure the quality of deliverables still meets your standards.

Through her growing network, Tina is constantly getting requests for services she doesn't offer. While she doesn't like turning down business, she's also hesitant to increase the scope of her offering and responsibilities.

You may eventually reach a point where you have too much work to handle while respecting the boundaries you've set up. Or this was part of your business model all along. Either way, during this chapter we'll discuss the benefits and responsibilities associated with hiring employees, freelancers, and virtual assistants.

Remember: Focus on Your Zone of Genius

I once spent two hours trying to format a PDF. I wanted all of the pages to be horizontally orientated except for one page that had a graph on it. This task was clearly a lot harder than I anticipated. Eventually, I gave up and found someone to do it on Fiverr. I paid them $20, and they sent it back to me in about ten minutes.

It was a painful lesson, but it stuck with me. I'm never going to be an expert at creating PDF's, and I don't want to be. I should have just hired someone else to do it in the first place. As a business owner, I feel that my time is better spent performing more critical tasks that others can't do. So is yours.

In this case, I would have been better off writing an insightful blog that provides value to my audiences and reinforces myself as an expert. Or, I could have made an explainer video showing exactly how to use one of the many tools I leverage on a daily basis. These two actions could have led to me interacting with more prospects, some of which eventually turned into clients. Either way, creating a PDF wasn't the best use of my time.

You have a gift, which is information that a defined audience needs and values. Again, this is your zone of genius. You'll want to actively avoid and outsource anything that takes you out of this zone.

Here's an easy way to wrap your head around it from a financial perspective, even if you don't charge by the hour.

If you make an average of $100/hour, outsource work that you wouldn't pay someone $100/hour to do. Even if you pay them $20 to do it, you're still banking $80 that hour since you can concentrate on something else.

There are several "rules" you can put in place to make sure you're doing the most impactful work, but it all comes down to one moment. Anytime you're thinking, "This isn't the best use of my time," consider that a trigger to delegate it in one way or another. Let's walk through a few ways you can outsource work to maximize your time.

tip

As a general rule, anytime you come across a task more than twice that isn't within your Zone of Genius, try to outsource it or manage it by some sort of tool or app.

Hiring a Virtual Assistant

I blog on a regular basis, and so should you if you want to build your brand as a consultant. Creating this content involves me operating in my zone of genius. Posting the blog on my website, not so much. I know how to use Squarespace, and it only takes about 15 minutes to post a blog once I've written it, but that's not the best use of my time. My virtual assistant (VA), Talia, handles this task on my behalf. You could take the same approach. You can create your content in Google Docs, then post the link to it in a Google Sheet. In this same sheet, let your VA know what tags to use, and link to any images you may want included. Once they do the work on your behalf, they can then mark it as resolved, giving you the opportunity to review before it's posted on your site.

You could also use a VA to post your upcoming workshops and events. Again, this something that only takes a few minutes but is easy to neglect when you're focusing on other high-priority activities. However, speaking to an audience is one of the best ways to land new clients. Not letting people know where you'll be appearing has a direct impact on your sales funnel and, eventually, your revenue. A VA saves the day by adding all this information to my website.

Your virtual assistant can also research and compile contact information for podcasts you want to appear on, organizations you'd like to partner with, and events you may want to speak at. This information is incredibly valuable but also time consuming.

These are just a few of the tasks VAS can do. Others include:

▶ Entering data
▶ Organizing your to-do list and calendar
▶ Booking travel arrangements

▶ Setting up your email marketing program and managing your list

▶ Coordinating the technical aspects of leading a webinar

▶ Creating content to share on your social media accounts

▶ Engaging with your followers

You may be initially hesitant to get a VA. You may not want to spend the time vetting someone, or be concerned they may not work out, even if they made it through the screening process. You can take a shortcut through this process by asking your network for referrals. My approach was very basic: I just put up an Instagram Story asking if anyone was currently working with a VA who had additional availability. Fortunately, I got a response, and that's how I was connected to a qualified VA. You can try the same approach on LinkedIn as well. The goal is to get introduced to someone you can trust.

There are many websites you can look at, too—upwork.com is one of the most popular. You can view potential skills, work history, ratings and more.

Leveraging Your VA

It's important to remember, no matter how good your VA is, you won't get good results if you don't provide them with the right information.

One time in college my roommate and I were in the dining hall. The person working there asked him what he wanted and he replied, "I'll just take a hamburger." He was shocked when she put a hamburger on his tray, with no bun.

You can expect the same results from a VA, as well as other people you work with. By design, they tend to take things literally, so you'll want to be very clear. If they "mess up," there's a good chance it's your fault, not theirs.

I document all my requests via written text and video. I use Loom to record my screen and show my VA exactly what I need them to do. Beyond that, I give them the overall context so they can understand why I'm asking them. Often, they'll follow up with another process that may be more suitable.

Too often, people underutilize their virtual assistants. It's tempting to just do things yourself so you can get it over with. Or perhaps you don't want to spend time figuring out what you want them to do. In the long run, this is a mistake. You should fully leverage your VA by hiring them for a predetermined number of hours per month, which will force you to keep them busy by giving them various tasks.

It's helpful to give them ongoing tasks that take a long time to complete or can never be completed. Here are a few easy examples.

Getting Links to Your Website

As we discussed earlier, getting other sites to link back to you is a great way to boost your SEO. Your virtual assistant can proactively reach out to these sites on your behalf, which is called a *link-building campaign*. As mentioned, these other sites need to reflect a similar theme or audience. You also need to have a valuable piece of content that provides value to their target audience.

For example, a digital marketing consultant could create a guide called "10 Easy Ways for a Small Business to Increase Website Traffic," then have their VA share this content with chambers of commerce throughout the U.S. There are roughly 4,000 chambers of commerce in the U.S. with at least one full-time staff person and thousands more established as strictly volunteer entities. Clearly, this task would take a long time to complete.

Your VA would be responsible for finding the contact information for all these chambers. You may ask them to focus on specific cities or states, since you can easily land clients from this exposure.

You'll be responsible for creating the copy they would send. Here's a template for your reference:

> *I imagine many of your members would like to increase their website traffic but are short on time or are intimidated by digital marketing in general. To help solve for this challenge, I created a guide,* 10 Easy Ways for a Small Business to Increase Website Traffic. *Is this something you'd be interested in sharing with your members?*

If you use HubSpot, you can have this come from your email address, and you can handle any responses yourself. You may find they have a few questions, which would be better handled by you as opposed to your VA.

Here's another way you could use the exact same list but potentially create an even larger opportunity:

> *I imagine many of your members would like to increase their website traffic but are short on time or are intimidated by digital marketing in general. To help solve for this challenge, I created a guide,* 10 Easy Ways for a Small Business to Increase Website Traffic. *Is this something you'd be interested in sharing with your members? I'm also available to lead a free 60-minute webinar where I'll dig deeper into the content and answer any questions your members may have.*

Just like that, your virtual assistant has put your lead generation on auto-pilot.

Working with Freelancers

You may choose to work with a freelancer or contractor to expand the scope of your services or allow you to spend more time on other activities.

As you read in Chapter 2, enlisting the help of freelancers has its advantages. You can charge a client $2,000 for part of a project, then pay a freelancer $1,000 to complete it. However, it's very important you align with freelancers that have the same commitment to excellence as you do. If possible, vet these individuals by getting references and looking at examples of their previous work.

If this weren't part of your original business plan, you'll want to carefully consider how it could impact the momentum you've already created. Ask yourself:

- ▶ Do you have time to manage people?
- ▶ How would you handle it if they left abruptly?
- ▶ Are you OK with trusting other people's work?

If you're a control freak, that last question may be challenging to answer.

It's also important to remember you're competing for the freelancer's time. They could easily come across another project that's more lucrative while you're sitting around wondering why they won't respond to your emails. This is why I don't recommend negotiating the fee a freelancer charges. You want them to feel happy with their compensation. It's also beneficial to keep them busy, if possible. Or be honest about how much work you'll be able to give them. They're running a business as well, and they will appreciate this transparency.

If a freelancer has access to any client data or accounts, you'll want to let the client know in advance. Anna Vatuone, the personal brand strategist, has freelancers help build Squarespace accounts on behalf of her clients, which she openly discloses. If not, a client could easily see a random person has access to their account, which would be a huge red flag.

Hiring a Full-Time Employee

Bringing on an employee comes with the same pros and cons as hiring a freelancer and whole lot more. You're starting a long-term relationship with this person, so you'll want to choose wisely. Unlike a freelancer, it's more challenging to cut ties with a full-time employee in most states. You may end up paying severance or unemployment and/or justifying why you let them go. Of course, this is a worse-case scenario, but it's something to keep in mind.

Your employees will likely want benefits, such as insurance and paid time off. Not only can this be costly, but it can also be time consuming to manage from an administrative standpoint. Managing employees also comes with a host of other questions to answer:

▶ Do you have a system in place to track time off?
▶ What's the policy for requesting time off?
▶ How many sick days do they get?
▶ How much can they spend on employee meals?
▶ Can they expense their travel to the office?
▶ Can they work from home?

You'll most likely need to get them a computer and any other gear needed to do their job. If they work with you locally, you'll need to pay for their desk or possibly get a bigger office. There are also many not-so-obvious fees, such as paying for two licenses for one product or another. I strongly suggest modeling out all these additional costs and considerations before determining if you want to move forward. You'll also need to determine how much you can pay. It's important to reward people for quality work, but you need to keep an eye on your expenses at the same time.

Along with overall management, keeping your employees happy and fulfilled will become part of the job. They may look to you for mentorship and need your understanding if they go through any personal challenges that may impact their work. As you can imagine, this is all time consuming and may distract you from operating in your zone of genius.

Don't forget about the upside as well. Having a dedicated full-time employee allows you to comfortably expand the scope of your current offering. You can also leverage them to grow your business. Consider offering some sort of incentive to them if they refer a prospect that turns into a client. Some agencies even offer a revenue share or commission on top of a guaranteed salary.

No matter how well you do at managing employees, you'll eventually have to deal with turnover. However, don't let that fear hold you back from empowering them.

Why This Is Important

While some people dream of having a large team to manage, and the revenue that comes along with it, there's a trade-off involved. You'll spend less time performing impactful work for the people you originally planned on helping and more time on management and administrative activities.

However, with the right team and systems set up, you could get to a place where you have the ability to step away from the day-to-day activities of running your business and explore other areas of interest. This could involve business development through speaking and content creation. Or something more personal such as volunteering, traveling, and just spending time with your family.

Action Items

▶ Keep notes on activities you're doing that aren't leveraging your zone of genius, consider leveraging a VA.

▶ Based on your experiences, consider whether or not you want to expand the scale or scope of your business.

▶ Before taking on a full-time employee, carefully consider the pros and cons associated with management.

Additional Revenue Streams

N ow it's time to think about more ways you can maximize the impact of your consulting business by adding more revenue streams. One way to think about your business is like a bike tire in which you have a central hub (in this case, coaching), and the spokes all connect to it but are slightly different.

Let's use Tina as an example.

Tina now has a steady flow of leads coming in. She's attracting the right prospects through her referrals, writing, and public speaking. A recognized expert, she was recently asked to speak at an event but had no idea how to respond when they asked what her rate was. She also notices people continually ask her what books she's reading, or how she stays up-to-date with everything in her industry. Some of these people would be a good fit for her consulting services, but they just can't afford her rate.

You'll eventually encounter some or all of these scenarios. This chapter describes how you can leverage your industry knowledge through other revenue streams including group coaching, online courses, and affiliate marketing. Paid speaking engagements are another great way to leverage your expertise, while actively prospecting more clients. This chapter will also cover how to get you on stage.

Group Coaching

Consulting on a one-on-one basis allows you to provide bespoke input to specific problems. Unfortunately, it's challenging to scale revenue with this approach. Outside of bringing on help, you have two options: increase your rates, or take on more work.

There's a limit to how much you can charge and still get a sufficient number of clients. Taking on more work makes sense at first, but your goal should be to build your business around your life, not the other way around.

Offering group coaching is a great way to scale your time while also making your services available to people who may not be able to afford your one-on-one rate.

Let's say you charge $1,000 per month as a retainer for your services. You could also offer group coaching at a cost of $400 per month. If you have five people in the group, you'll make $2,000 per month.

As a best practice, you'll need to carefully screen anyone whom you accept into the group. Members are paying for you to lead them and curate a good community. You may find they're supporting each other while you play the role of moderating. For this reason, it's important not to admit people just because they can afford it. You'll need to make sure they're a good cultural fit. For example, people who are too quiet don't provide value, while people who are too needy or disruptive have a negative impact on the environment.

Although this is group coaching, you'll want to make sure each member gets individual attention. In my group, we call these Huddle Seats, which is an opportunity for each member to chat about what they have going on while receiving feedback from the group. I also offer an initial one-on-one onboarding call so every member can get clear on their goals for the next 90 days and come to the group prepared to work.

Issues and thoughts can come up between meetings. As a best practice, form a private Facebook or Slack group so members can continue engaging outside of calls. You're still there to moderate, but these are largely group-driven conversations.

A common question that comes up is, "What if they all decide to start their own group for free?" Yes, this could happen, which is why your goal is to provide so much value that they don't want to. For example, you can record each session or bring in guest speakers to provide value. You could also offer a private coaching session to each group member every 30 days or so. Let's take a look at the structure you can follow to keep your group on track.

Weekly Team Meetings

Each week, a group of five business owners will meet to discuss their goals, progress, and roadblocks. You can conduct the video calls via Zoom or another online meeting platform.

Here's a detailed example of how you could structure your weekly group calls.

Commitment:
▶ One-hour weekly video calls.
▶ Each member gets a ten-minute "Huddle Seat" on the call.
▶ Full attention on the call; no multitasking.
▶ Document and update your weekly goals/accomplishments.

Call Agenda:
▶ Three-minute welcome
▶ Ten-minute first member "Huddle Seat"
▶ Ten-minute second member "Huddle Seat"
▶ Ten-minute third member "Huddle Seat"
▶ Ten-minute fourth member "Huddle Seat"
▶ Ten-minute fifth member "Huddle Seat"
▶ Seven-minute open discussion

Total meeting time: one hour

Structure for Huddle Seat:
▶ What were your goals for last week?
▶ Did you hit your goals? yes/no
▶ What did you learn?

- ► What are your goals for this week?
- ► What could cause you not to achieve these goals?
- ► Brainstorm, questions, or feedback.

Again, you can leverage Google Sheets or Asana to track the goals and progress of each team member.

Over time, you may discover this approach is more lucrative and manageable than offering one-on-one consulting. While you can still choose to do so, I suggest raising the price of your one-on-one consulting and steering more people toward the group model. One-on-one consulting may be a better solution for your more advanced clients, while the group model may work better for those who need with the basics.

Another advantage of group coaching is that it can accelerate your learning curve in regard to professional development. Again, let's assume you have five people in your program and it lasts 60 days. You'll learn something new from each person you coach, and taking on five at a time is great way to learn more during a shorter period of time. Beyond that, provided you do a good job, you'll be able to acquire five testimonials and multiple referrals by the end of your program.

I strongly suggest considering this when you're first starting out.

tip

If part of your marketing strategy includes free webinars, this provides a great opportunity to mention your group coaching offer. Participants have already been exposed to how effectively you can communicate remotely and may have gained value from connecting with their peers online.

Online Courses

The lure of "passive income" prompts many consultants to create an online course. While it's great to have something your audience can buy that doesn't involve any additional time for you to deliver, the process is anything but passive.

Creating a course involves:

- ► Determining what content to include
- ► Recording videos
- ► Developing templates and worksheets
- ► Setting up your online course platform
- ► Building an email list
- ► Promoting your course
- ► Making any needed updates

After all this, many course creators struggle to make back the time and money invested in making the course. Teachable (www.teachable.com) is an all-in-one platform that helps you create and sell courses online. They also have numerous resources, including a guide to help you successfully launch a course.

A good online course idea will meet these criteria before you start creating:

▶ There is an audience for it.
▶ It's narrow enough that you can get granular in how you cover your content.
▶ You are an authority on the topic.
▶ You've gone back and validated your course idea.

Launch Your Course

Here are the basic steps you can take to launch an online course.

Find an Audience for Your Course

You can't sell a course if you don't have anyone to sell to, so your first step will be finding an audience. Fortunately, you've already finished this step.

Become a Thought Leader

More than growing your audience, you want to become a thought leader in your niche. This means you are going to try to become one of those go-to people that your target audience seeks when they have a question. The content you've previously created will come in handy here.

Use Your Audience to Choose a Course Idea

Once you've become active in the online communities where your audience hangs out, you can begin figuring out what their pain points are and what online course topic would best serve them. The enrollment calls you've had with prospects will prove invaluable here. Questions become content. What questions do you repeatedly hear that you can answer by creating online content? Think of ten topics you could speak on that would solve real problems.

Niche Down Your Course Idea

Once you've got your list of ten course ideas, it's time to start getting into nitty-gritty and deciding on the one transformation you want for your students. It might be tempting to say, "I'm going to create the ultimate supreme course to digital marketing," but it's unlikely that you'll actually be able to pack every single thing anyone will need to know about digital marketing into one, easily consumable course. Instead, narrow it down. Create a course on how nonprofits can leverage digital marketing. Or best ways to leverage digital marketing for lead generation. An online course should be a shortcut to an outcome, and you're better off if that outcome is a tangible change your audience will be able to notice.

Use Lead Magnets to Grow Your Audience

Again, this is something you may have already done, so you should be in a good spot here. However, it's important to nurture your audience with good content before asking them to buy something. You can also consider making a lead magnet that specifically refers to the content covered in your course. This way, you'll be sure to attract the audience who is looking for the answers you'll provide. If you're making a digital marketing course for nonprofits, an ebook, "Ten Content Marketing Strategies for Nonprofits," would be a great fit.

Validate Your Course Topic

The process of validating your course helps you ensure that your hunch that this is a topic your audience would be interested in is spot on. Validating your course idea can be as simple as sending an email to your audience, or a thorough process that involves preselling and marketing before actually creating your course.

If you've already built an audience and an email list, validating your online course idea could be as simple as sending in an opt-in to your email list.

Let them know you're working on creating an online course, and, if they're interested in being in your first round of students, to click the link you'll provide and sign up for a segmented email list where they can get exclusive deals when your course goes live.

If you don't have an audience yet or you're really trying to be sure that you're on the right track with your online course, you can try promoting a presale. If you're not familiar, a presale is when you put your course sales page live before you've finished creating your course content.

In either case, if there's not enough interest to justify building the course, there may be a few reasons why:

▶ You're marketing to the wrong audience.
▶ You're marketing the wrong course idea to the right audience.
▶ You haven't successfully justified why they need the course.

In your case, it's most likely the second. Consider following up and asking what they would like to see in a course you offer. If you hear a common theme around a few specific topics, go through this same process again to determine which option is best for you. Just be sure it's a topic you can speak to effectively.

Once you've decided on your topic, you'll need to plan your course content. This will be somewhat similar to the process you went through when determining your signature speech.

Create Your Course Structure

First, in regard to your course, reflect on your audience's current understanding of this topic. Next, write down everything they need to learn, in order, to reach the outcomes you've promised. This part can be challenging. Since you're the expert, it's easy to gloss over some of the details that seem obvious to you. The more input you provide, the more likely they are to reach their goals.

Once you've created a list that is thorough, you can start grouping like steps into sections or modules.

Create Your Video Outline

Your video outline will be even more granular than the course structure you've created. You'll dive into each section step by step. Imagine you're teaching someone how to assemble furniture from IKEA. I strongly suggest using this opportunity to write a script. You may know this stuff off the top of your head, but you'll be able to add more structure and clarity if you write it all down.

Decide How You'll Present Your Content

Would you like to present a slide, talk to the camera, or do both? Some things are easier to show than explain. In this case a talking head video would be preferred. Or you may want to make things more personal by starting with a talking head video before sharing your screen. For detail-oriented tasks, especially if the student will be completing them on a computer, you'll definitely want to share your screen.

Be sure to notate your choices now so you'll be ready to record when the time comes.

Plan Supplemental Materials

Since you won't be teaching this live, your students will need some sort of interaction. Workbooks, checklists, and quizzes allow students to interact with the content in a more personal way. These bonuses can often be the tipping point when someone is deciding whether or not to buy your course. You can also choose to have an online community, such as a Slack or Facebook group. Again, this is a huge bonus, but you'll also be responsible for moderating content and answering questions. If you go this route, be aware of how much time you may spend maintaining this group.

Now it's time to actually record your content. In many cases, you can do so with the equipment you currently have, but you can also opt for a professional studio and team. Again, Teachable has resources to help with this on their site.

Paid Speaking Gigs

Becoming a paid speaker is an incredibly efficient way to generate revenue and leads.

Figure 14–1 shows a rough breakdown of how much you can expect to earn.

New speaker	$500 to $2,500
Beginning speaker, just establishing brand	$2,500 to $10,000
Established speakers with social proof	$10,000 to $20,000
Those who are very well known	$20,000 to $35,000
Celebrities and household names	$50,000 to $300,000

FIGURE 14–1: **Speaking Gig Income**

I made $3,500 for my first speaking appearance. An event organizer in Texas saw me speak at an event in New York. Although I didn't get paid to speak at the New York event, it was obviously worth my time.

In most cases, you'll have to deliver some speeches for free before you get paid. Speaking at coworking spaces and smaller local events is a great way to get these reps in. We discussed this earlier, so you may already be in a good spot here.

You may be able to record some of these smaller events and create a speaker reel. Your speaker reel is a video highlighting the topics you chat about while also proving your ability to effectively speak. These are typically between two and three minutes long. While you don't absolutely need one to land paid speaking gigs (I didn't have one before landing my first few), this will greatly increase your chances of getting booked and paid to speak.

Another way to increase your chances? Don't wait for organizers to approach you. This was my biggest challenge initially. I was able to book a fair number of gigs, but I didn't have a strategic process to grow my business. You can avoid that mistake by following the process I've outlined below.

Be Specific

Determine where you want to speak and who you want to speak to.

If this is purely a revenue-generating opportunity, you won't be as concerned about landing leads while speaking. However, if you want to use this as a lead-generating opportunity, you'll want to be more specific about where you speak. A medical organization once asked me to speak at their conference. This isn't my target audience so I requested a rate much higher than I normally would have.

Do you want to speak at a local venue, or are you willing to travel? Traveling opens more opportunities but also complicates things. It's challenging to get work done on the road, and it will most likely disturb your personal life. Sure, you may be getting paid $2,500 to speak at a conference, but you may get behind on client emails and miss a few workouts while on the road. You'll need to determine how much the event and your travel time is worth to you.

Would you rather speak at conferences or private organizations? Conferences are a great way to get your name out there, but they often don't pay as much as private organizations. In some cases, you'll only get your travel, lodging and event ticket comped. If this is the case, make sure your target audience will be in attendance. Private organizations include professional events, nonprofits, and universities. These aren't open to the general public and typically pay better. However, they may be less likely to let you record content for your speaker reel.

Start Researching Opportunities

Start off by Googling "Your topic + conference." For example, "sleep conference."

You'll see results right away and can start making a list. If you have a VA, I recommend asking them to handle this step. If you're willing to travel, try entering other cities you may be interested in visiting. For example, "sleep conference Seattle." You may notice conferences that have already taken place show up—that's totally fine. If this is an annual conference, you can still reach out to the event coordinators to see when they're booking speakers for next year. Before you do, take a look at some of the topics covered. This will give you an idea of what they were looking for in the past. This isn't to say you should try to speak on the same topics, but you'll get an understanding of how to describe your talk and may provide you with an opportunity to expand on a previous topic.

Contact Event Coordinators

Now that you have all your information gathered, it's time to reach out. You're used to this by now, and can follow the same approach we outlined in Chapter 10. As always, be sure to respect their time, and make it clear you've done some research in advance. The main difference here is you know they most likely need speakers for their event.

Hello {Name, if available}

When will you be taking speaker applications for the upcoming XYZ event?

{Provide three to four sentences on who you are, what you speak about, and how you can help their audience with your message.}

Follow up a few days later. If you don't get a reply, wait another week and follow up again. If there is no answer, wait until the event is a little closer and try again.

Ideally, you should be reaching out three to six months in advance. Some events book out longer, some shorter. This is why you need to contact decision makers with plenty of notice.

If you do hear back from the organizer, get them on the phone as quickly as possible. This is where your online scheduling tool will come in handy. They may be reaching out to several speakers, so you'll want to lock things in as quickly as possible. Here are a few questions you should ask during the call:

- ▶ Who is the target audience?
- ▶ How many people will be attending?
- ▶ What's the transformation they're looking to get from attending the event?
- ▶ Is it also possible for me to connect with attendees one-on-one through a workshop or roundtable? This will be music to their ears. It proves you actually want to have an impact on attendees.
- ▶ Do you need help finding additional speakers? Keep in mind, the event organizer probably isn't a subject-matter expert. You'd be doing them a huge favor if you can help out here. Plus, it gives you an excuse to reach out to other speakers, who may be able to help you down the line.
- ▶ What is your speaker budget? They may straight up tell you, or ask what your fee is. Make sure you have a target fee in mind before hopping on the phone! Of course, they may have no budget at all.

Remember, if you're just starting out, you'll most likely need to speak for free. Even as an established speaker, it may sometimes make sense to do so. These are some things to consider if the organizer doesn't have a budget or is otherwise unwilling to pay you.

When to speak for free:

- ▶ You're just starting out.

▶ You already have content prepared.

▶ Your target audience will be in attendance.

▶ You don't need to travel.

▶ High-quality video or pictures will be made available.

The last factor is a huge bonus, especially if it's a video. You can use this content to create or augment your speaker reel. It can also be repurposed as social media content.

Seal the Deal

The final step is sending over a speaker contract or replying to the one they send you. You can find a sample speaker contract on my website at terryrice.co/bookresources. Get this done as quickly as possible.

If you want to be taken seriously, you'll need to set up a separate speaker website or at least have a section on your website that references your availability as a speaker. You can take a look at mine for reference at www.terryrice.co/speaking. Jason Feifer, editor-in-chief of *Entrepreneur* magazine, has a great speaking page for you to explore as well at www.jasonfeifer.com/speaking.

Speaking about your signature topics on podcasts or writing about it on your blog will reinforce your expertise. Most organizers don't want a custom speech—they want your best speech. You can swap out a few examples to make it relevant to the audience, but you shouldn't be writing each presentation from scratch. Having a solid grasp on your content will also help alleviate any nervous feelings that may creep up.

On that note, if you have challenges with public speaking, it's important to remember everyone in attendance is there to learn from you. They want you to do well because they're genuinely interested in what you have to say. So, this isn't a hostile situation—you have an audience full of allies.

Affiliate Marketing

I mentioned an upcoming conference while I was teaching a class at General Assembly. A few weeks later, a student reached out to me and thanked me for the recommendation. She went to the conference and gained a great deal of value from it. Tickets to this conference started at $1,900. I couldn't believe she decided to attend simply because I casually mentioned. That's when I began to realize the influence that came with being a recognized expert. I then started noticing students would start taking notes as I mentioned books I was reading or other certifications I completed. After a while, my next step became pretty clear: I needed to start generating revenue through affiliate marketing.

The best definition of what affiliate marketing is can be found on Pat Flynn's Smart Passive Income (www.smartpassiveincome.com/): "*Affiliate marketing* is the process of earning a commission by promoting other people's (or company's) products. You find a product you like, promote it to others, and earn a piece of the profit for each sale that you make."

You Find a Product You Like

This part is super important. Your audience trusts your opinion, which is why they may potentially spend money on something you're promoting. But you have to actually like it. Don't just start promoting random products to make a buck. It's inauthentic, at best. I typically promote books, apps, and gear I use to run my business (www.terryrice.co/resources). For example, I appear on podcasts frequently, so I have a high-quality microphone. My goal is to help other people in my position, but it's important to be overt about the fact I'm using affiliate links.

The following information is posted on my website:

There are a lot of great resources available to grow your business, and it can be overwhelming to know what to use or where to go. To make it simpler, I've assembled my favorite books, apps, and gear. This is your toolkit for running a successful business.

Please note that some of the links below are affiliate links, and at no additional cost to you, I will earn a commission if you decide to make a purchase. I have experience with all of these companies, and I recommend them because I find them to be helpful and useful. However, do not spend money on these products unless you feel they will help you achieve your goals or save you time.

Not only is a disclaimer the right thing to do, but they are also mandated by the Federal Trade Commission. You can learn more about the specifics on the FTC website (https://www.ftc.gov/tips-advice/business-center/guidance/ftcs-endorsement-guides-what-people-are-asking).

If you'd like to generate revenue through affiliate marketing, here are a few things to consider:

▶ *What products are you already recommending to your audience?* Check to see if they have an affiliate program. A simple Google Search "product +affiliate program" should give you this information.

▶ *How would you like to present the use case?* This can be a blog or explainer video.

▶ *What is your revenue goal?* If you'd just like to try it out or pay a few small bills, there's no need for an in-depth promotional strategy. If you're looking to generate larger amounts of revenue, you'll need to consider an SEO and/or social media promotional strategy.

You can also join affiliate networks, which act as an intermediary between publishers (affiliates) and merchant affiliate programs. You'll be able to browse thousands of companies and apply to be an affiliate on the same platform.

Here are a few affiliate networks to consider:

▶ PeerFly (https://peerfly.com/)
▶ ShareASale (https://www.shareasale.com/)
▶ Rakuten (https://www.rakuten.com/)
▶ Amazon Associates (https://affiliate-program.amazon.com/)

You'll be more successful if you're promoting to an audience that already knows, likes, and trusts you. Because of this, your email list will be an extremely valuable resource because you will be selling to your known audience. However, some affiliate programs (including Amazon Associates) only allow affiliate links on websites. You can mention whatever you are promoting in your email, but the actual affiliate link would need to be on your website. Regardless of the program, make sure you pay attention to all regulations. It's not uncommon for affiliates to be removed from program for violating terms of service, even if they're generating a large number of sales.

Keep in mind, you'll be getting a percentage of the sale price. Most affiliates pay from 5 percent to 30 percent. Of course, 5 percent of a $1,900 conference ticket is a lot more than you would get from promoting a book, so you'll need to be strategic about what you decide to promote. Are you looking for a large volume of sales, or a large payout from a smaller number of sales? Generally, a mix of both is ideal.

Lastly, you don't need to make thousands of dollars per day to be successful. I made $8 my first week as an affiliate and was happy to have it cover the cost of my lunch. I think of affiliate revenue as a way to pay small, specific bills, such as my children's daycare.

Referrals

You can't (and shouldn't) say yes to every prospect or lead you come across. Instead, you should seek to monetize these opportunities by connecting them with another service provider. In exchange, you can ask for a finder's fee or referral fee. This is very popular in the legal and real estate industry, but some professionals feel uncomfortable doing so.

First, you should only refer people who are good at what they do *and* have solid morals. Meaning, they won't rip you off when it's time to pay the referral fee. It can be challenging to enforce these agreements, and it's probably not worth your time in the long run.

Next, you'll need to chat with them so you can qualify and quantify the benefit of entering a referral partnership. We'll use Tina to illustrate how this conversation could flow:

Tina: Omar, you did a great job building my website. Are you currently looking for more clients?

Omar: Absolutely. I love building websites. Finding clients is the only part of the job I don't like.

Tina: Glad to hear you have bandwidth. What part about finding clients do you not like?

(Notice how she's asking probing questions to qualify his need for help.)

Omar: Well, first of all, I feel somewhat desperate when I'm posting on LinkedIn or sending cold emails. Even if I do get someone on the phone, I feel like I have to prove myself over and over again before I can get an understanding of what they need. After that, a lot of people just aren't ready to move forward. They think they can just spend more money on Google Ads and call it a day.

Tina: Wow, that does sound frustrating. So, it would be great if you could get in front of people who were ready to make a financial commitment and already appreciate the value of your work, right?

Omar: Yes! I could save so much time and focus on doing what I'm actually good at. I spend around five or six hours per week promoting myself. I'd much rather be doing revenue-generating work.

Tina: OK, so I have an idea. I come across a lot of companies that need to streamline their business process. Beyond that, it's obvious many of them need help with their websites. I bring this up to them, but it's not a service I offer. Would you be interested in partnering with me, where I would send you these leads, and you pay me a percentage of any deals you close?

Omar: Absolutely. I respect your work and I know you're connected in the small business community. What percent were you thinking?

Tina: That's great to hear. Does 15 percent sound fair to you? If you send me some information on your services and a rough estimate of how much you charge, I'll be able to prequalify people before sending them your way.

Omar: Sounds like a plan. You'll save me a great deal of time, and I'll appreciate the fact you've already vetted them.

In regard to the fee, anywhere from 15 to 20 percent is average. If this is an ongoing service, you may determine the fee only lasts for a predetermined amount of time, such as the first three months. Another option is to do a flat rate. For example, one of my colleagues pays $500 for any lead that converts.

You may not generate a large volume of revenue with this approach, unless you're actively seeking opportunities. Either way, it's a nice way to make money by simply connecting two people via email.

Why This Is Important

With all these opportunities available, it's easy to feel like you're not focused. It's important to remember, you're still monetizing your knowledge. Your expertise is the hub of everything you do; these additional revenue streams are just spokes, allowing you to take advantage of different channels and approaches.

In fact, you're most likely leaving revenue on the table if you don't explore additional revenue streams. You may find some of them are a better fit based on the time, lifestyle, and financial freedom you desire.

Action Items

▶ Consider which additional revenue streams are the best fit for your area of expertise and lifestyle.

▶ If you choose to pursue paid speaking, set up a "Speaking" page on your website and consider creating a speaker reel.

▶ If you choose to do affiliate marketing, consider creating explainer videos for the products or services you promote.

▶ Carefully track the revenue generated from each revenue stream as compared to the effort involved, and make adjustments as needed.

The Game Within the Game

Tina's business is continuing to grow month over month. It's by no means easy, but she has a defined process that brings a steady flow of leads and she can comfortably navigate the associated conversations. She's also working with some amazing clients, and they're largely happy with her service. Although things are going well, she still feels anxious about the future. She also gets slightly irked when she loses out on opportunities she thought she was guaranteed to win.

There's still something missing from Tina's journey, and it may be the most important to yours: mindset training and a dedicated wellness routine.

You can't maintain a successful business if you don't maintain your mental and physical health. This brief chapter covers techniques for living a high-performance lifestyle and making more thoughtful decisions.

It can be easy to dismiss this chapter as fluff. You may want to start diving in and getting clients on the phone. Don't make that mistake. This training is what separates good entrepreneurs from the great ones. We'll now cover how you can be the best possible version of yourself, however you choose to define it.

Get in the Zone

Distractions, both good and bad, will come up out of nowhere, but it's vitally important to live in the present moment. You can't focus if you're constantly thinking about what previously happened or what could happen. For example, during enrollment calls, I used to find myself thinking about what I was going to say next instead of being present and listening to what the prospect was saying at the moment. I eventually adopted a simple trick to help with that. Whenever I feel my mind drifting, I wiggle my toes. This literally tells me where I am ("be where your feet are") and reminds me to focus on the present moment. You can win or lose a big opportunity just based on how much you're paying attention. Have you ever not been paying attention to someone, then tried to join back in, hoping what you said made sense? Me too, it's not fun, and my response doesn't make sense the majority of the time. Even if it's marginally acceptable, I won't be revealing wisdom or expressing high performance.

Focusing on the present also allows you to quickly recover from any setbacks you may encounter. Undoubtedly, you're going to lose a big deal or get turned down for a major speaking opportunity. Sure, it's unfortunate, but the faster you can recover, the faster you can focus on appreciating and creating other opportunities.

However, you shouldn't feel like you always need to be doing something. Focus on being, and let the doing come from there. This part can be hard to wrap your head around. *Don't I get paid for doing stuff?* Well, yes and no. You get paid for being someone who provides value to a defined audience. Providing this value might include reading a new book, attending a seminar, or even heading to a yoga class so you can clear your head. As a result, you may end up writing some brilliant article that gets you a few new clients or speaking opportunities. This same article may catch the eye of a podcast host who invites you on her show, giving you even more exposure. See, none of this happens if you're constantly doing something, even if it's revenue generating. This is why I rarely do hourly work, even if the person is willing to pay my rate. I'd rather learn or express something that can earn me tens of thousands of dollars as opposed to a few hundred.

Be Patient and Strategic

One benefit of having revenue goals is knowing when to stop generating revenue. Well, at least short-term revenue. Again, this may sound counterintuitive so I'll provide an example. Let's say your two-year plan involves generating 50 percent of your income through passive revenue streams, such as an online course. During the interim, let's assume your monthly revenue goal through consulting is $10,000. Once you've hit your goal of $10,000 in monthly recurring revenue from consulting, you can stop taking on more work so you'll have time to complete your online course. I know this can be hard because I've been there myself. In 2019, I turned down $60,000 worth of work so I could focus on revenue streams more aligned with the lifestyle I wanted for me and my family. Fortunately, I was able to make that money back, but more importantly, I was able to spend more time with my kids.

You'll have to make the same tough decisions. Should you speak at an online conference that will add 1,000 people to your email list, or make $1,000 doing a small project? Well, if your long-term goal involves selling that course, 1,000 additional email subscribers would most likely be the better option. Even if you sell the course for $300, and 1 percent of people on your list buy the course, you'd make $3,000 from those additional emails instead of $1,000 for the small project.

This is just one example of why having patience and developing a long-term strategy are essential to maintaining a successful and fulfilling consulting business.

Positive Self-Talk

With the uncertainty and isolation that comes with entrepreneurship, it's easy to get down yourself from time to time. You may have friends or former colleagues who have stable 9-to-5 jobs while you're constantly hoping a contract gets signed or a budget gets approved. If you find yourself thinking negatively, that's a trigger for your positive self-talk to come in. Remind yourself of all the challenges you've overcome, all the clients you've helped, and all the great opportunities that you're setting yourself up for. It's important to frontload these thoughts by documenting them and repeating them on a regular basis. Sure, you may not have a steady 9-to-5 job, but you have the opportunity and autonomy to support yourself on your own terms and the lifestyle that comes with it.

Self-confidence comes from within. Be sure to celebrate every small victory as it comes and get ready for the amazing experiences awaiting you.

I wish you the best of luck on your journey!

About the Author

Terry Rice is a business development consultant in Brooklyn. As the founder of Terry Rice Consulting, he helps entrepreneurs monetize their knowledge without sacrificing their health, family, or personal interests. His focus is advising professionals on how to launch or scale their knowledge-based businesses, which can include consulting, speaking appearances, online courses, and associated revenue streams. Terry is also an adjunct instructor at NYU where he leads workshops for career-driven individuals. A recognized digital marketing expert, his previous experience includes helping clients achieve their business goals while working at Adobe and Facebook.

Acknowledgments

Writing a book is harder than I thought and more rewarding than I could have ever imagined. I'm grateful for the inspiration, support, and feedback of several friends and advisors including Jason Feifer, Todd Johnson, Jennifer Dorsey, JJ Smith, Dorie Clark, and Mike Koenigs.

I'd also like to thank everyone at Entrepreneur Media and General Assembly for their valued partnership and for always treating me like I was part of the team.

Finally, thanks to my wife Domenique for her unrelenting support. Her patience and encouragement—even through the most challenging times—made all of this possible.

Index

Printed in the USA
CPSIA information can be obtained
at www.ICGtesting.com
JSHW051552230824
68671JS00014B/186

9 781599 186658